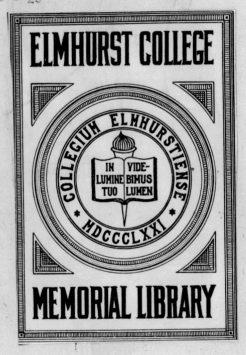

THE SOCIAL WORK OF CHRISTIAN MISSIONS

The Social Work of Christian Missions

By

ALVA W. TAYLOR

Professor of Social Service and Christian Missions in
The Bible College of Missouri

CINCINNATI
THE FOREIGN CHRISTIAN MISSIONARY SOCIETY
1912

PREFACE

THIS volume is designed for those who are interested in the humanitarian phases of Christian missions. The paramount interests of our time are social. Foreign missions furnish an inexhaustible opportunity for social endeavor, and contribute annals in social progress such as are being written in no other field of human endeavor. It is the hope of the author that this volume may be a source of information and inspiration to those who have been aroused by present-day missionary movements among laymen, women, students, and the young people of the Churches. It is especially designed as a help to mission classes in schools and churches. For those classes that desire a short series of studies the introduction, the six chapters, and a review will furnish a division of material; for those who wish a series of lessons extending over a longer period, one or more sections can be used for each assignment. The sources for the work are enumerated in a bibliography at the end of the volume. An especial debt is due Volume III, of Dr. Dennis, great work on "Christian Missions and Social Progress," in the writing of sections 2, 3, and 4 of Chapter

5

PREFACE

V, and to Dr. Williamson's little volume entitled, "The Healing of the Nations," in sections 3 and 4, in Chapter III, and to Volume VIII, of the Edinburgh Conference Report, in section 3 of Chapter VIII. I am grateful to my colleague, Professor Charles E. Underwood, for assistance in revising the manuscript.

CONTENTS

INTRODUCTION

CHAPTER I

CHAPTER II

7

CONTENTS

CHAPTER III

CHAPTER IV

CHAPTER V

CONTENTS

CHAPTER VI

ILLUSTRATIONS

INTRODUCTION

THE SOCIAL TASK OF MISSIONS

1. THE MISSIONARY AS A SOCIAL FORCE.

Christianity is the religion of humanity. Jesus most often spoke of himself as the Son of Man. In the use of that term he desired to identify himself with humanity. He was God's idea of a man. In his humanity we find one of the divinest factors in revelation. There is little danger that the Church will lose sight of his divinity. It has ever emphasized his oneness with God the Father, but it has not always so emphasized his oneness with men. If we have not a divine Christ we have no Christ, but if we lose the human in Christ, we lose his power to reach the world. The Apostle's great desire for his followers was that they "might rise to the fullness of the stature of manhood which is found in Christ Jesus." To be a perfect man is to be Godlike. It was to that perfection of manliness that Jesus wished to lift the world. And true Christianity goes into the world to create manhood and womanhood. But Christian manhood is never selfish; it "seeks not its own, is not puffed up." Jesus would save the world by making men the saviors of their kind. There is no salvation except through service. The Christian individual is socialized. In-

11

dividual power without social conscience is the most dangerous weapon to put into mortal hands. The writer who said it was worth while to fertilize the fields of Europe with the blood of millions if thereby one Napoleon could be created, expressed the very antithesis of Christianity.

The socialized individual is the real working factor in the world's uplift. A materialistic evolution may sneer at the missionary and at all benevolence, but a Christian evolution sees in benevolence the most active factor in the civilizing process. When Emerson described civilization in terms of woman's power and influence, he only described it in terms of benevolence, for it is the spirit of altruism that overcomes selfishness and compels man to give womankind their rights. The progress of civilization can be told in terms of altruism and the processes of socialization. Strong individuals may be developed by the "struggle for self," but society advances through the "struggle for others." This "struggle for others" is the law of Christianity. It is the ferment of social service that is leavening the world with good. Christian personality is not that of the "superman," but that of the great-hearted lover of his kind; it has an "enthusiasm of humanity," the power to see the viewpoint of others, to sympathetically enter into their lives and to lift them up. The missionary is the model of Christly aspiration in his faith in humanity's potentiality, and in his self-forgetting determination to lift up the lowest of men.

The Kingdom of God is a new social order. It is a Republic of Humanity, a realization of the life of

INTRODUCTION

God in the society of men. Jesus said his mission
was "to give life and to give it more abundantly."
To give life one must give the things that make life
worth while. He can not give life to the slum and leave
the slum, nor can he take it to the heathen world and
leave the world heathen. Shakespeare said, "He who
takes the prop to my house takes my house." The
goods of life are its "props." A man's life does not
consist in the abundance of the things he possesses, but
his possessions in terms of habit, custom, ideas, homes,
friends, environment, and ideals are so much a part
of him that the worth of the lives of men are largely
measured by the value of such possessions. The Kingdom of God is to be rooted into the earth. The task
of Christ was to save the world, not merely to save a
few out of the world. The "kingdoms of this world
are to become those of our Lord and his Christ." He
would save commerce to honesty and a true social
service; politics to purity and as the chief bond of
communities in their fraternal life; religion to human
service and as the strongest factor for binding the peoples of the earth together. The Kingdom of God is to
include all nations and peoples in a social bond that
will put an end to strife and bloodshed, and bring peace
to all the earth. It is to so reorder human relationship that all men will be privileged to dwell in a democracy of right, where there will be no tyranny, no
expropriation of the things of another, no class privilege, and no deprivation of opportunity to him who is
worthy. Its ideal may be millenniums away, but vast
strides have already been made toward it, and if one
has faith in the eternal purpose and might, he can not

13

INTRODUCTION

doubt the final issue. But men are "to be workers together with God," in bringing these things to pass.

A theological Christianity has failed to save the world. The saving power of Christianity has ever been its interest in men and its faith that the fact of Christ, once planted in their hearts, would accomplish the task. We must have a theology. It is only a systematic statement of our knowledge and theory of divine things. But sociological Christianity is our knowledge and theory at work. Henry D. Lloyd called it "organized friendliness." In the middle ages it was thought an acceptance of the creed was sufficient unto salvation. Peoples were given the choice of the dogma or the sword. St. Olaf went through Scandinavia, singing psalms and coercing by the sword, until he had "Christianized" the land. Charlemagne sent priest and soldier together, and our Anglo-Saxon forefathers accepted death by the thousands rather than take that kind of "salvation." Great bishops used the pomp and awe of ceremonial, and lured with promises of escape from torment by mere submission to baptism and an abandonment of the idols. St. Xavier sprinkled drops of water on the heads of multitudes in Goa and reported tens of thousands of conversions; ringing his bell, he would call the crowds together, and the simple message, "be baptized and you are saved," found little opposition; but he left no better life behind him. Charlemagne established churches and schools, and lifted up the converted masses somewhat, but his converts were mostly "baptized pagans," and Europe was Christian in name only. The same story is written in the history of Latin

14

Reading Room in Y. M. C. A. at Tienstin, China. The Association is spending $2,000,000 enlarging its foreign work.

America. It is yet starkly heathen for the most part. There was no social message; Christianity did not mean the implanting of new ideals of society. It is in its social message that Christianity outruns the other missionary religions in its permanent power to uplift, and in the measure that it has implanted social principles, has its missionary message taken the rootage among a people that brought permanent success. It becomes a civilizer through its implanting of humane principles and social ideals in the hearts of its converts, and they leaven the whole of the life about them. Immediate conversion is not always the means of doing the best work. The planting of the Kingdom of God may be slow, but it will, in the end, bring forth its fruitage in the greater abundance if it is securely planted. No true missionary despises numbers, neither does he count names on the church roll his success; his gauge of success is that of regenerate lives and the building up of a community of regenerate folk, with all the endowments of modern Christian civilization. A civilization can not be lifted by speculation or by a syllogism, and it was never lifted by a legend. It is not our theories about Christ, but our implanting of the life of Christ, with all it means to our civilization in higher ideals, purer thinking, better homes, greater equality, more value on life as such, a higher standard of living, and more of the spirit of service, that brings the world to him. When we "take chemists for our cooks, and mineralogists for our masons," we will put our dependence in a theological Christianity to save the world. "The old creeds are not fitted to harmonize with the intellectual, social, and moral

15

power of the modern world," says Mr. T. E. Slater, of India.

The new-born society of the missionary community means problems in dress reform, in housing, in hygiene and sanitation, in education and the art of healing, in more democratic relationships, a new family order, in the readjustment of the place of womankind in society and the home, and, in time, in railroad building, international commerce, diplomacy, and all those arts of social intercourse that characterize civilization at its highest. Through these arts of socialization and civilization the missionary confers upon all the society about his Christian community the social blessings of his gospel. He thus lifts all into a more proximate relationship to his gospel, and shortens the step they must take in order to come into the Kingdom. Then he may hope for true "mass conversions." Most men move with the crowd; they think and act together. When all custom and thought is lifted near the Christian level, multitudes find it possible to join the Christian host.

2. THE SOCIAL WORK OF THE MISSIONARY.

The missionary is the pioneer of all progress among the nations to which he goes. Following the method of his Master, he goes to change the hearts of individuals, and when he has changed their hearts he has so changed their attitude toward all life that he has inaugurated a new era in their midst. The change he makes in them is such that all better things are a part of their future quest.

The social question is simply the question of the

other fellow. Its final solution rests in the Golden Rule and the caring for things of others as if they were our own. Heathenism cares little for the other fellow. It has no charity worthy the name; it knows little of self-control in appetite, temper, or ambition; its gods are selfish, and its passions are intemperate; its conceit is monumental and commensurate only with its ignorance; each seeks that which is his own, and the fates may take the hindmost. There is little social welfare attempted by paganism; Christianity alone rests upon social service.

Like his Master, the missionary goes to give a more abundant life. He creates within man a desire for the larger things, and so adds to their lives that living becomes a new thing to them. It has been said that when a savage is converted, he immediately wants a stool, a suit of clothes, and a book. The first is the symbol of all those implements of domestic art that make for home and domestic comfort; the second stands for decency, courtesy, and virtue; the last is the beginning of education.

Let it be here said that the missionary does not go to impose an American type of architecture or tailoring, nor to make any peculiar Western custom of living the distinctive type of the new manner of life. He is not sent to Anglicize or Occidentalize, but to create a new heart and to reorder native customs according to the dictates of cleanliness, both within and without. When he has created the new creature, he needs but to lead him in the cleansing and repair of his ancient habits of life, and a rebuilding according to the environment in which his lot is cast, and by the

2 17

best use of the material that fortune has placed at his hand. It is not the missioner's part to change racial customs, except where they are hurtful. He is there to build up a nationalism, and create a patriotism that is peculiar to the people to whom he has gone. It is not his task to plant a foreign flag, nor is he the emissary of commerce, though his work opens the pathway for the trade of all industrial peoples.

The new aspiration is the beginning of all things new. Bishop Colenso was a brilliant and benevolent man. He reasoned, however, that as in religion is the quintessence of human attainment and refinement, it could be best taught after a barbarous people had learned some of the arts of civilization and been brought by education to a state where they could appreciate the high things of the spirit. He accordingly went to the Zulus with industrial schools, and offered them better houses to dwell in. They looked on with awe, but did not see why they should adopt the white man's house or implements, and made little attempt to imitate. Two humble and unlearned Dutch missionaries had founded a mission a day's journey away, in the simple faith that if they could create a new heart in the black man, all these other things could be added. They taught heart and hand together. After some years of effort, Colenso rode across to their mission one day, and throwing a bag of fifty golden sovereigns on the office table, said, "You have won." Samuel Marsden tried to put the material arts of civilization first in New Zealand and, after twenty years of trial, confessed his error in method; within a single generation the whole people were transformed by putting

first things first and creating a new life within the
savage Maori breast. When Christianity had found
lodgment in the heart of the savage Africander, he
nursed his benefactor, Robert Moffat, with the tender-
ness of a woman. The French gave the Arabs stone
cabins, and the proud, old sheik thanked them for
so excellent a shelter for his sheep. The Canadians
built cedar huts for the Chippewas of the Northwest,
and they herded their dogs in them, while they held
to the immemorial custom of freezing in wigwams.
The missionary went to both, and by creating a new
desire, taught them to build their own houses. Wherever he goes, the nomads build fixed habitations, the
warlike become tillers of the soil, the piratical learn
the arts of industry, and the slave-holding come to
honor labor.

Buckle lays it down as an axiom in the philosophy
of history, that progress comes from within—it can
not be conferred as a gift, it must be won out of a desire that will fit for its attainment. It is for that
reason that men, who, like Sir Andrew Frasier, have
been colonial administrators for thirty years, testify
that Christian missionaries do more than all the power
of an empire can do to regenerate a nation.

No more effective testimony to the social benefits
of Christian missions could be given than the contrast
between two villages—the one heathen and the other
Christian. In the heathen village the garbage is
in the street, the houses are in a more or less tumble-
down condition, the roofs are awry and full of leaks,
the children run naked, the women are in rags, dirt
is omnipresent, vice is written on most of the counte-

19

nances, hoplessness overcasts the faces of the many,
and absurd custom, with its counterpart of superstition, is everywhere rife. In the Christian village the
house may be no larger, but it will be clean; the toil
may be little more remunerative, but it will be more
persistent; the children will be clothed, and the women
neat in native garments; the village street no longer
reeks with filth, and an angle of uprightness has seized
upon things; faces take on a new light, hope is in every
countenance, and superstition has given place to an
enlightenment that is in striking contrast to the old
manner of living and doing. The ribaldry of heathen
song has given over to the quiet of Christian cheer,
the riot of heathen sport has surrendered to the orderliness of Christian pleasure, and in place of the vile
rites of superstition comes an enlightenment wherein
instruction in righteousness and temperance is made
to worship God.

The missionary's home is a social settlement in
the midst of a pagan community. There he exemplifies
the improvements that civilization offers to humble
natives, and shows forth the heart of it in the art of
Christian living. There woman is honored and children accorded rights that heathenism has never recognized. On these two facts the arch of civilization's
triumph is founded, and the key of it is Christian love.

The missionary translates books on every theme
that relates to human welfare, and opens a new world
to the astonished eyes of ancient half-civilizations.
He inaugurates philanthropy and heals the bodies of the
sick and provides for the lives of the abandoned and
teaches the blessed art of caring for one another. The

old barbaric heartlessness is supplanted by a touch of mercy, and self-immolation and mutilation give way to deeds of fellow-help. He plants schools and is to-day actually instructing more than a million and a half of the youth of pagan lands. From these come the makers of to-morrow in every heathen nation. Through his institutions of learning in China, the whole empire has changed immemorial customs of instruction. Verbeck taught the makers of the new Japan and founded the Imperial University in Tokio. The industrial schools at Lovedale and Blantyre have been multiplied into hundreds, and from each goes forth a roll of men with new hearts, trained minds, and skilled hands, ready for the practical work of starting civilization. Education and philanthropy become the web upon which Christianity, by the hands of the missioner, weaves the woof of a nation's life into a new fabric. He is the only foreigner there with no exploiting aim, but only to do the people good. For a time he may not be comprehended, and may often have to suffer for the judgment others have begotten in the native mind for all men of his color, but in the end he is understood and multitudes arise to call him blessed.

Missionaries have done more than evangelize, translate books, found schools and hospitals, teach industry, and preach the gospel by a model home life and a character that is upright. They have advised governments regarding important innovations making for progress and peace. They have added to earning power by invention, and have introduced revolutionary ideas in commerce and agriculture.

INTRODUCTION

They have overcome hurtful customs in the name of comfort and humanity, and opened new avenues for adding to the material welfare of the people. They have taught native races the value of untouched resources and the waste of uneconomic habits. There has been no boon that could be given that they have not given, and in their delivery of a religious message they have ever counted that any gift made to the intelligence, comfort, cleanliness, neighborliness, earning capacity, or any other means of social welfare, was a part of their work and an honor to their Master, who went about doing good.

Heathenism has never valued life highly for its own sake. For that reason suicide has been easy, and the murder of infants frightful. Christian missions puts life in the scale of values and finds it of supreme worth. The missioner has gone where cannibalism was openly practiced and has abolished it; slavery has yielded to his persuasion on a hundred mission fields; infanticide has become a crime wherever his hold has been established; woman has been raised from the position of a chattel to that of a companion to man in the ratio that his message has been adopted, and woman owes more to the missionary than to any other active factor in the world of affairs. Customs that have been a torture to the flesh and signs of subservience have been abolished, worship has been turned from the insanities of mutilation and ascetic denial to the sweet reasonableness of praise and prayer and the help of fellow-man.

Suspicion is a species of social paralysis in heathendom. Where there is no fellow-trust there can be no

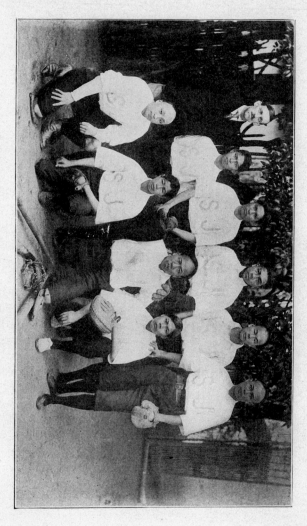

Baseball Team of St. John's University, Shanghai, China. The Chinese boys make fine athletes.

fraternal bond. Trade is not conducted there in trust, but in distrust; it is not so much the normal means of building up the economic life as it is a subterfuge for preying upon your kind; it is a species of knavery under a flag of truce, so to speak, for it is a battle of wits and a warfare of deceit. Government is for the sake of those who have the power rather than for the sake of the governed, and "justice is sold for a bribe and the poor for a pair of shoes." Few men trust their neighbors, and every man is regarded as a rogue. The missioner establishes the virtue of fellow-trust in his convert and makes him a man worthy of trust. Upon this virtue the solid fabric of a better order of society is builded, and from the ranks of the missionary's pupils governments and commercial houses select men for their trustworthy agents. The growth of the Christian community in the midst of a native population strengthens the bonds of credit and proves by degrees that honesty is the best policy. Administration in the hands of native Christians gives the subjects of law a taste of integrity in government, and raises the demand for the same uprightness among all officials.

Certain philosophers of history once urged the theory of the hero as the creator of progress. To-day we have a revision of that theory in favor of the group, who in the midst of mankind become a leaven of new ideas and better customs, and from whom arise the leaders and the teachers of a better day. They think out better ways in an interchange of ideas and exemplify their ideals in their own manner of living and doing. This is democracy's revision of the monarchical theory of the hero. This is the process of the missionary evangel in its social work. Christian missions create a new manner of life among groups of natives and they become a leaven in the whole lump, illustrating to their fellows the benefits of the new way of living. From these groups flow out streams of influence that redeem the whole land in the course of time, and bring multitudes to accept the creed of civilization.

To raise the standard of life among a people is civilization's finest achievement. It is one of the most patent of the results of the missionary propaganda. To add to the life of a whole nation by making the daily lives of all its people somewhat more worth while, is, by that much, to bring nearer the Kingdom of Heaven. To level the inequalities even a little, and to bestow the gifts of mercy, justice, and humility upon the ideals of a nation, is to do the work of Him who came to make all men brethren. Christian missions proceed by creating this man and that a new creature—not to save them out of the world, but within it and for its sake. They live the new and better way and a great multitude come to appreciate it. The passion of fellow-help is implanted, and each does something for the other. The leaven of human good is spread far and wide, the spirit of social service creates a new and better order of society, and the Christ, thus lifted up, draws all men unto himself.

The figures that tell the number of converts, inspiring as they are, tell but a part of the story of the boon of good the missionary evangel carries unto the uttermost parts of the earth. They are really but an index to the mighty volume of good the missionary is doing. "Teaching them to observe all things, whatsoever I have commanded you," he creates a new order of society.

3. CHRISTIANITY AS THE UNIVERSAL FAITH.

All nations have possessed a national religion. Old Roman statesmen were personally filled with contempt for the gods, but held to them because they deemed them means of holding the people in reverence and an aid to order. They did not dream of a state without religion. Modern Japan illustrates the same national intuition. Shintoism is the religion of patriotism. The worship of the emperor comes down from primitive legends that trace the birth of the dynasty to the gods. Roman Christianity was thrust out of Japan because it was thought to be interfering with the emperor's divinity, and that its fealty to the pope would divide the loyalty of the people. Confucianism is Chinese. It is nationalistic in its claim to their fealty. The emperor is its supreme head. It has spread to other Mongolians as an ethical creed, but China has exalted Confucius to divine honors and requires all officers and all students at governmental schools to pay him religious reverence. Brahmanism is Hindu. It has never spread beyond the borders of India, and has no desire to do so. Buddhism has become largely Mongolian. Burmah and Ceylon are about the only non-Mongolian peoples who make it their faith. It was once a missionary faith and its early annals furnish heroic examples of missionary zeal, but it had not the vital social power to keep it

25

to the task. Its contact with Christianity has aroused a small revival among Japanese Buddhists, and they are adopting elements of the Christian gospel in an effort to overcome its inroads. It to-day has fewer adherents than has Protestantism, numbering, according to late authority, only 184,000,000, though it has been living 2,500 years amid great populations. Mohammedanism is essentially Arabic. It is a missionary religion, but centers in Arabic nations and among the descendants of Arabs, and has ever been as much political as religious. The great Moslem population of India is traceable to the Arabic invasions of centuries ago, and its adherents are largely their descendants, mixed, it is true, with the less virile Hindu blood. The same is true of the faith of China.

The missionary sterility of all these religions is due to a lack of social force. A faith spreads in the ratio that it gives men an interest in fellow-men, and inspires them with the spirit of service. When a religion is frankly nationalistic, there is no missionary appeal. Unless it puts great value upon life as such, and assesses the world in which we live at divine values, there will be little missionary enthusiasm. Confucianism makes every man sufficient unto himself. It allows concubinage, and thus the degradation of womankind. Slavery is practiced and suicide is very common. The criminal code of China has ever been barbarous, and there has never been either universal education or a charity worth the name. The great sage said, "Thou shalt love thy friend and ignore thy enemy," and added, "Have no friends not your equal." His version of the golden rule made it a negation.

INTRODUCTION

The ethical code of Confucius is a great gain over that of nature religion or of Hinduism, but it lacks the propulsive power of faith in God and a universal interest in man. It ignores the Creator and teaches that the less said about him the better. Buddhism began in benevolence, but is to-day existing with no charity beyond the giving of small alms in order to acquire merit. Its monks are lazy and generally ignorant, though among them are found some who are in earnest and seek the light. But Buddhism crushes desire as bad and turns its true disciples from the world as from a place of evil. It has made little real contribution to progress, and its hope for life is that it may end in extinction. Brahmanism is a caste religion. That within itself is sufficient social condemnation. Mohammedanism has been the most virile of non-Christian missionary religions, but its propaganda has been by fire and sword and thus by anti-social force. It teaches polygamy and concubinage, and practices slavery. It makes of its followers a superior caste wherever they dwell, and comes to all other faiths with fierce intolerance. Its fatalistic theology must destroy its missionary force whenever it is separated from political aims. Its missionary crusades have ever been political and never humanitarian.

Christianity is the great universal religion. It has been misused by half-converted adherents for every end that human desire might conceive. There are yet those among them who would make it racial, and deny that it has any efficacy among others than the whites. They have accepted it from Asia, and from alien hands, then deny that it is fit for either Asia or

aliens. It has proven what its founder intended it
to be—the greatest social force in the world. It proclaimed that life was valuable for its own sake. When
Jesus asked, "Of how much more value is a man than
a sheep?" he challenged the world's pagan view of the
value of humanity. Man is never to be considered
property nor made subservient to property rights.
When he called the body the temple of the spirit, he
laid a sacred value on the flesh and taught none to
despise the world. His call to service was a heroic
demand for complete self-forgetfulness, not to avoid
the world and its frictions and temptations, but to
grapple with evil boldly and valiantly to overcome
it. When the Apostle Paul said there was neither
Jew nor Greek, bond nor free, male nor female, in
Christ, he propounded the essential democracy of
Christianity; in the first he abolished all racial and
nationalistic aversions; in the second he condemned
all class distinctions; in the third he raised woman to a
level with man and destroyed the age long, universal,
anti-social, discrimination against her. Christianity
is a dynamic of all just action. The institutions of
civilization are its enginery, but its religion is its dynamic, its propelling force. Gov. Woodrow Wilson
defines Christianity as the center of education, philanthropy, science, politics, philosophy, and, "in
short, the center of all sentient and thinking life."

The manner in which it makes good in its missionary propaganda is twofold; it wins great numbers of
individuals and creates them social factors for the uplift of their kind; and it leavens the social and moral
life of whole populations that it has not yet won to

membership in its churches. As illustration of this latter, Japan furnishes a brilliant example. A Japanese Buddhist, a physician, says, "Christian morals have won in Japan." Dr. Nitobe, author of Bushido, says, "Christianity alone is powerful enough to overcome the materialism and utilitarianism of Japan." A Japanese Buddhist priest said, "Christian ethics are the best in the world." A Buddhist professor of ethics says, "Japan must accept Christian ethics." Professor Murakami, Japan's greatest Buddhist scholar, acknowledges the moral superiority of Christianity. Baron Mayajima says: "No matter how large our army and our navy, if we do not build upon righteousness we shall fail. The religion of Christ is the one most full of strength for the nation and for the individual." Prince Ito, within the last few years, said: "The only true civilization rests on Christian principles. The young men who receive Christian education will be the main factors in the future development of Japan." Count Okuma said to a body of young Christians, "Live and preach this (the Christian life), and you will supply just what the nation most needs at this juncture." The Japanese Minister of Education recommended the New Testament as the first book for all young men to read. A volume of such statements might be compiled from the leading minds of all lands. The religion of the Nazarene knows no national lines; its principles are universal, they touch all humanity where it is at one, and in time will lift all humanity to that oneness which will banish "man's inhumanity to man," for "the spirit of Christ is the spirit of Humanity." It binds to no dead past, as

INTRODUCTION

does Confucianism, but builds solidly upon the past; it forgets not the world to find God, as does Brahmanism, but finds God in his world; it loses not God to find the good of mortal life, as does Buddhism, but gauges the good of mortal life by his divine life; it conquers not by a sword of blood, as does Mohammedanism, but by the sword of the Spirit and the bonds of peace. It would make all men brethren, still all hate, break down all sectism and class discord, and rule the world through the constructive power of a universal love.

Religion is the mightiest of all forces resident in humanity. Men die for their faith when they would for nothing else, and their lives are controlled by it against all the powers of being. "Man is incurably religious," said Paul Sabbatier. Spencer failed utterly to find the non-religious man his theories hypothecated, and Ratzel, in his "History of Mankind," affirms that there is no such thing as a non-religious human being. Even the skeptical, in their very aversion to religion, display "incurably religious" interests. Christianity rises to its highest in its hold upon the fealty of its followers. Moslems may die in fanatical zeal, but "the power of the love of Christ has been displayed alike in the most heroic pages of Christian martyrdom, in the most pathetic pages of Christian resignation, in the tenderest pages of Christian charity," says Lecky. The power of Christianity as a civilizing force is manifesting itself in these latter days as never before, because its followers are moved to-day with a better understanding of the genius of their faith. Their conquest is by the subtle

30

art of persuasion. That art has ever been like the
warming rays of the sunshine in its power to fructify
life. Like the acorn that bursts the rock, Christian
lives rend the Gibraltars of heathenism. Æsop's
fable told how the sun took the coat off the traveler's
back when the violence of the wind only made him
hold it the more closely. "The Apostle Paul's journeys outrivaled in significance to civilization the conquests of Alexander and Cæsar," says Prof. William
Ramsey. "The missionary has done more for the
Levant than all the nations of the earth together,"
said Gladstone. "Bulgaria would never have gained
her independence had it not been for Roberts College," mourned the late Sultan Abdul Hamid. "Not
England, but Jesus Christ is redeeming India," says
Sir Andrew Frasier, for thirty years an administrator
in India. "England has sent out a tremendous moral
force in the life and character of that mighty prophet
to conquer and hold this vast empire. None but
Jesus, none but Jesus, ever deserved this bright, this
precious diadem, and Jesus shall have it," cried Keshub
Chunder Sen, founder of the Brahmo Somaj, in an
eloquent peroration to an address he delivered in Calcutta. Religion is the mightiest social power resident
in humanity, and the Christian religion is the mightiest
power for the constructive uplift of mankind that has
ever entered the world.

CHAPTER I

Things Figures Can Not Tell

1. By Their Fruits Ye Shall Know Them.

"History is no sphinx." Wendell Philipps asked students of comparative civilization to allow China to speak for Confucianism, Japan for Buddhism, India for Brahmanism, Turkey for Mohammedanism, and America for Christianity.

The final test of a culture, a civilization, or a religion is the progress it creates. Every great religion produces a civilization, and every civilization has a religion at its core. Christianity creates personality; it appeals to the individual; then it socializes him. Christian personality is not measured in terms of selfish self, but in the terms of unselfish self. It vaunts not itself, is not puffed up, seeketh not its own. The greatest personality is that which most adequately sees the viewpoint of all its fellows and most ardently sympathizes with all mankind, and then adds a mastery of those events that may be ordered for the common welfare of all.

"Religion works most fruitfully through the social organism," said Dr. Storrs. It makes good in social terms. History reveals that it is not in material things, but in moral character and social good that civilization finds its guarantee of stability. Good

3   33

becomes the "goods" of civilization. Economics are selfish. Property rights, when made the paramount consideration, bias the minds of men to things rather than to human good; competitor is arrayed against competitor, class against class, and nation against nation. Human welfare demands co-operation. Christianity creates high social ideals and gives men the will to realize them. A religion is powerful to the extent that it interests men in men, and gives them the working means of advancing the welfare of their kind.

Christianity courts the tests of comparison as a ministrant of social good and an inspirer of social progress. Lowell defied the skeptics "to point to any spot ten miles square, where a decent man could live in decency, supporting and educating his children, where age is reverenced, infancy protected, manhood respected, womanhood honored, and human life held in due regard, where the gospel of Christ has not gone and cleared the way and made decency and society respectable." Frederic Dennison Maurice said, "Every one is sensible of a change in the whole climate of thought and feeling the moment he crosses the boundary which divides Christianity from Heathendom." Christianity alone is flexible enough to meet the demands made by human progress. It creates in man a desire for better things, and gives him the open mind and makes him a "seeker after truth," promising that in that truth he shall find the freedom that all souls seek. Not all Christians keep the open mind, but they do keep it in just so far as they are Christians. And it is not merely a wearing of the name Christian, nor

34

*O*ld Examination Stalls at Nankin, China. Modern Civil
Service is now replacing the old-time examination in
Classics.

A Modern School on the site of the Old Examination Stalls
at Chentu, West China. This illustrates the New Era
in China.

the fact that one has appropriated part of the benefits of Christianity that gives the world a helper. Open-mindedness and truth seeking are necessary conditions of Christian progress.

Paganism is static; its Golden Ages are in the past. Christianity puts its Golden Age in the future. The Kingdom of God has not yet reached its consummation, it is *to* come. Pagan religions give men the backward look. Christianity gives them the forward look. Men are optimistic because they believe their age has made progress over previous ages. Paganism is pessimistic because it believes the present is worse than the past, and therefore the future will perhaps be yet worse. Paganism hopes to escape this world, to retire into oblivion, or to be rescued into a better place. Some Christians have adulterated their religious doctrines with these ideas, but at the heart of Christendom has ever been found a saving faith in the promises of Scripture for a "new heaven and new earth."

China is the answer to Confucianism. Confucius pretended to give nothing new; he pointed back to the sages that were old, even in his time. He gave China the finest ethical code found outside the Christian Scriptures. But the Celestial Empire has made no progress in a millennium. Hers has been the backward look. She worships her ancestors. All things were done as the fathers did them. The ethical code of Confucius's five relations lifted her as high as ethical precept could lift a great people. Then, notwithstanding the fact that the Chinese are among the most virile, industrious, intellectual, and peaceable of

35

peoples, China crystalized and progress ceased. The ethics of Confucius is negative. It lacks a propulsive power for social good. Confucianism solidifies, Christianity fructifies.

Japan is the answer to Buddhism. The religion of Gautama is the most spiritual outside of Christianity. The great Buddha was himself one of the first of saints. Yet to-day Buddhism is represented by a priesthood whose character is, to say the least, not synonymous with charity or virtue, and with a worship that does not imply any fundamental social obligation. Christianity has brought more progress to Japan in fifty years than Buddhism brought in five hundred years. "Buddhism is a personal philosophy rather than a social power," says Dr. Carver. Japan's social life remained licentious, her daughters were sold into shame, woman was not a companion to her husband, and despotism ruled in all her life, from the family to the throne. It was not until Christian ideals entered Japan and she opened her eyes to the arts and powers of Christian progress, that she threw off the provincial customs of ages and entered the list of modern nations.

India is the answer to Brahmanism. A Greek traveler and historian of twenty-five hundred years ago draws a picture of Hindu social life that agrees with their own traditions of better days in the past. According to his account there was then no caste, and the customs were less cruel than they were when the first missionaries arrived, two centuries ago. Buddhism came before that ancient date and sought to lift India out of a semi-animistic faith to a higher

36

realm of philosophy and of religious meditation. But Brahmanism overcame the purer teaching, and there is every evidence that it has been a degenerating, rather than a regenerating religion. Caste paralyzes all power for social progress, because there can be no real progress without the enlarging of democratic ideals and the realization of a larger amount of social equality. Woman is in a more abject state in India than in any land outside of savagery. Their worship is conducted with debasing practices and through forms that testify to degeneracy of ideals. India has kept no annals except such as her religious traditions have preserved. Her dominating religion, which should have been her social force, has been more nearly anti-social. Instead of uniting the nation, it has tended to disintegrate it. It has had no positive evangel. It has been eclectic, and adopted and absorbed and then debased almost every better religion or philosophy proposed in that benighted land. If it was said of China that she was not a country but a race, it could be said of India that she was not even a race, but a heterogenous collection of peoples, fenced in by the giant Himalayas, curiously cultivating at one extreme a speculative metaphysic, and at the other slowly losing vitality through anti-social customs.

Turkey is the answer to Mohammedanism. The faith of Islam was created out of a degenerate Judaism and some stray snatches of early Christianity, and then adapted to the life of Arabs. It took on the military spirit and became missionary through desire of conquest. It has a legalistic moral code, a sensual promise for the hereafter, a strong, prejudicial sect

37

spirit, and an unelastic social ideal. It has no caste, but it is a caste within itself. Its legalism prevents it becoming a leaven for moral welfare, for legalism does not have power to create real character, not even a Christian legalism. It is fatalistic, and therefore deprived of the dynamics of progress, even though it had the moral power that high principles would give. The answer of history to Moslemism is the contradiction of a medieval nation in close contact with the world currents of progress, and yet denying ingress to their fructifying tides. Turkey is to-day apparently turning to modern ways, but she is doing so at the cost of her historic religious position. The Sheik-ul-Islam is repealing her sacred traditions and denuding her of her battle-cries, and proclaiming the hated "infidel" and "Christian dog" a brother. The young Turks are men who received their education in a Christian atmosphere. Christian missions set the models for Turkey's proposed school system, and cultivated the minds of so many of the youth that when rebellion broke over the ramparts of tyranny there were none to defend the old regime, and the land was leavened with enough of a citizenship to make a modern government an immediate and practicable reality. Islam created no school system, but it did create a harem. It brought no gospel of peace, but boldly practiced one of conversion or extermination. It did not open, but defiantly closed and prejudiced minds. It plead a form of equality for the "faithful" and thus improved Hinduism, but it plead for intolerance toward all not of its creed, and it evolved no system of benevolence, founded no real homes,

38

instilled no ideals of justice or mercy or a humble walk with God. Its social power is not more than equal to its inculcation of those practices which Christianity teaches, and its denial of progress is to be discovered in those anti-social principles, through the practice of which it fails to reach up to the lofty ideals of Christianity.

The world to which Jesus came was no more moral, democratic, human, or charitable than is that to which his gospel is carried to-day by the missionary. How do we account for the difference between that world and the one which professes Christianity to-day? Christian civilization alone, among the civilizations of the world, has made great progress and seems to be even yet only in the childhood of its growth. It is not yet perfected, but its glory is that it is ever going on toward perfection. A thing is to be judged, not by its immature attainments, but by the promise it gives of fruitage and by the fruit it has already borne. There are many good things in the pagan world and there are many bad in Christendom, but the comparison is not in a confusing process of selecting the best and the worst, but in an averaging of the totals.

Our modern Christian civilization testifies eloquently to the success of Christianity as a civilizer. Our forefathers had been barbarians from time immemorial until Christianity was brought to them. From that time the evolution of modern Anglo-Saxon and Teutonic civilization began. To challenge the missionary is to deny the very courses of history. We have not yet purged ourselves of all our pagan heritage. We have a great deal of baptized paganism

39

in our churches. There is a great deal of counterfeit afloat, but its existence only evidences the value of the genuine. Christianity alone, among the great religions, has created benevolence and brotherly love and impressed them upon whole nations as ideals of life. It alone has created that type of personality which expresses itself in fellow-service. It alone expresses sacrifice in social terms, and makes religion a thing of service to fellow-man. It stands the test of the "average good."

2. THE STORY OF THE FIGURES.

Statistics are usually considered dry, but let it be a column of digits that sums up our profits or tells the totals of a fortune that has come to us, and we are aroused to a feverish enthusiasm. Figures that indicate a remarkable missionary advance ought to be very interesting to Christians, because they tell of new recruits to the cause, and much more, they tell of conquests that mean permanent territory added to Christian lands, and are eloquent with the romance of missionary adventure and the tragedy of missionary sacrifice.

There are a few critics yet that scoff at the missionary enterprise, but their ignorance is so coming to shame them that their dolorous and caustic voices are not often heard. No one but an intellectual provincial, a moral agnostic, a medieval race-hater, or a dogmatic religious quack could be cynical about an enterprise that brings so much of human good and shows such an amazing success as does the missionary enterprise. Every present-day Christian people have

40

abandoned an ethnic faith to accept Christianity, and the marvelous success of this first century of modern missionary activity gives assurance that every people with an ethnic faith will ultimately abandon it in favor of Christianity. It was a Jew that brought the gospel to Rome, a Roman that took it to France, a Frenchman that took it to Scandinavia, a Scotchman that evangelized Ireland, and an Irishman that, in turn, made the missionary conquest of Scotland. No people have received Christianity except at the hands of an alien, and it is at the hands of aliens who have been bereft of provincial conceit and filled with Christ-like confidence in men, without regard to race, color, or kind, that it is being taken to practically every land under the sun to-day. There is a patriotism of the Kingdom of God, and a fealty to the interests of humanity that makes a man none the less loyal to his own people, but fills him with a larger love for all the world.

The first million converts of the modern mission-ary era were won in one hundred years; the second million were added in twelve years, and the next mil-lion will be gained in six years. In China it took thirty-five years to win the first six, and at the end of fifty years there were less than a thousand who pro-fessed evangelical Christianity in that hoary old land; but at the end of the second half-century there are a round quarter-million in the Protestant Christian community there, and the numbers have increased sevenfold in two decades. In India the increase has been even more gratifying. In the first of three de-cades it was 53%, in the second 61%, and in the third

86%. Twenty-five years ago Korea was closed land, but to-day there are more than 200,000 who are either already baptized or are under instruction in preparation for that culminative act of Christian allegiance, and the numbers are increasing at the rate of 30% annually. Livingstone found Africa a "Dark Continent," but to-day the lights of a million lives shine around its shores and pierce into its interior. Whole nations, like Uganda, have been won from barbarism. In the South Seas the first band of heroic English missionaries were driven off the island of Tahiti only a little over a century ago. Up to the present that single little Christian island has sent 160 missionaries to the islands around about, and whole groups, like the Figis, have been Christianized. Uganda and the Figis, two of the darkest spots that civilization has ever entered, are to-day said to provide the largest percentage of regular church goers of any places in Christendom, and to be among the most peaceful lands known. In South India, the oldest of modern Protestant mission fields, and in one of the most difficult countries, the cumulative effects of the work is telling mightily, and gives promise of a greatly accelerated increase in numbers as the evangel attains the momentum brought by further years of success. The United South India Church alone numbers nearly a quarter-million members, while in all South India there are a half-million communicants in the church, and half as many more belong to the Christian community about the churches; in three years one Presbyterian mission has received no less than 3,000 converts. In Japan the numerical advance has been slower, but

42

the moral success has been out of all proportions to the numerical increase of the churches; there are only 70,000 Protestant church members, but they are increasing at the rate of 10% per annum. They are of the more potential classes, and exercise an influence in society and in the state out of all proportion to their numbers. It is claimed that a million of the educated youth of Japan hold the New Testament as the one authoritative ethical code, and order their lives by it quite as well as a like number that might be selected from our churches at home. There is on the foreign field to-day a Christian community of more than 5,000,000 souls, about one-half of whom have been received into active membership of the churches. Ten years ago there were but 3,500,000, and fifteen years ago less than 3,000,000. At the present rate of increase there will be another million inside the next six years, and many now living will have their eyes gladdened by the sight of a million per year being added to the Christian host that is so rapidly arising in the regions beyond the seas.

But, gratifying as the evangelistic statistics are, they do not tell all the story. Multitudes receive of the good the missionary offers that do not openly profess the creed he takes. There are 10,000 missionary homes, every one of which is a neighborhood center, doing, in a way, the work of a social settlement. There are 160 mission presses upon which there are printed 500 periodicals, besides tracts innumerable and thousands of books. Through the diffusion of literature, knowledge on every theme that forms a part of modern knowledge is disseminated.

43

Missionaries translate books of science, history, political economy, sociology, and law. They acquaint the backward nations with the progress of civilization, and put in their hands the knowledge and art essential to attain it for themselves. They conduct 25,000 schools and in them instruct more than 1,500,000 pupils. The instruction reaches from the kindergarten to the university and technical instruction. Through them they create a citizenship. In Japan the Doshisha alone has trained 6,000 native leaders for all walks of life. In Turkey instruction has been given to upwards of 40,000 annually, and when the new era came in a day there was a vast leaven of citizenship, instructed in modern learning, to hail the day with joy and to guide the uninstructed by the way of peace into better things. The missionary school became the harbinger of all the instruction modern India possesses, and set the model for both China and Japan. In the mission hospitals and dispensaries millions receive balm for their wounds and healing for their diseases, and, in the course of time, will bring to each nation a native medical profession, competent to care for its own ailments. A native ministry is being trained, and the mission church is more and more relying upon it. When there is a competent native leadership for the churches, there will be an advance such as no foreign leadership can ever hope to bring, for the people of every tongue listen most readily and follow most confidently their own leaders. An old society, like the London Missionary Society, illustrates the trend in this matter. With an income of a million a year, they employ but 295 mis-

sionaries, and have a staff of native workers numbering 4,000 under their supervision. Their fields were
among the first opened, and have been cultivated long
enough to develop a native leadership. The Christian communities under their care number 400,000
souls, and their statesmanlike policy is an example
to all younger mission boards. In the older South
India fields there are 900 missionaries and 14,000
native workers. Quite as promising as the development of a native leadership for the mission churches
is the rapid increase in self-support. To make comparison between the giving of mission churches and
those at home, the basis must be not that of dollar
with dollar, but that of earning capacity and the scale
of wages. The 70,000 Christians in Japan gave
$150,000 last year, and wages in Japan are but a frac-
tion of what they are in the United States. A most
conservative estimate would make that sum worth
a million dollars in American earning power. The
Korean churches pay 90% of their native ministry
and build practically all their own chapels and school
houses. The Ceylonese Christians give an average
of 36 days' wages out of each year for each member.
The Congregationalists are among the most liberal
givers at home, their giving being 50% higher than
the average for the home churches, and they give only
an average of eight or nine days' wages apiece per year
to all the work of the church, or one-fourth what the
Ceylonese give. The African converts in the Bolenge
field, on the Congo, give one-tenth of their income
as a minimum and add to it one-tenth of their membership as evangelists. In China the membership

has increased eleven times in thirty years, and the ratio of native giving has increased thirty times. The Telugus and Tamils of South India earn from eight to twelve cents per day and give $120,000 per annum. In 1900 the native churches on all mission fields gave $1,833,961. In 1910 they gave $5,249,405. Their contributions were trebled in a decade. In the same decade the home churches increased their missionary gifts by 80%, or a little more than one-fourth as rapidly as the mission churches. The mission churches are missionary to the last degree. They are not smitten with the smug and selfish and wholly perverted idea that the gospel is for them, or that there is any peculiarity of kind that makes them its beneficiaries, and rules out others as unfit or undeserving or as sufficient unto themselves. It is sheer atheism to talk about Christianity for the West, and contend that each people evolves the religion that is best for it. The West did not evolve Christianity; it received it at the hand of missionaries from the East.

The figures that tell of the awakened interest of the church at home are also inspiring. The Protestant Reformation began with an avowed hostility to missionary work. It has been only a century and a half since the first beacon light was sent to a foreign field, and for the first one hundred years little was done. We are now at the dawn of the missionary era. The church is awakened at last, and the interest of the past decade is eloquent with prophecy for the future. The total support has grown from $17,315,526 in 1900, to $32,139,509 in 1910, or an increase of almost 100%. The Laymen's Missionary Movement is essentially a pocket-book movement; it is an awakening of incomes to a responsibility of stewardship. The class that holds the purse strings are discovering in the mission fields spheres for investment that pay as do no others. The campaign was inaugurated in Toronto in 1908; that city's gift increased from $175,000 to $363,000 the first year, and went up to $411,000 the second. It is a fair index of the generosity the Movement is to bring, it means the most adequate financing of opportunities offered in the field that has ever been realized. The number of missionaries has increased by one-third in the decade, and the number of employed native workers by one-half. The missionary host is increasing at the rate of 3% per annum, but the opportunities are increasing at double that ratio. In the past four years the Student Volunteer Movement has furnished 1,275 new missioners, and has some 6,000 recruits preparing in the various colleges for future enlistment. Their increase over the past quadrennium was 27%, and was 64% over the one before the last. The church at home is awakening, but she is yet bestowing $12 per member upon herself each year, while sending only 40 cents to the mission field. She supports one minister for every 140 members at home, and wastes vast sums upon denominational enterprises that duplicate the Christian efforts of sister churches. She supports an ordained worker for every 400 people in the home field, and supplies one for every 200,000 in the lands that have no churches, schools, books, hospitals, or Christian homes, nor the mighty influence of Christian civilization. To-day there are on the field 21,248 missionaries and 91,513 native helpers, or a total missionary host of 113,207; ten years ago there were 91,899. To-day there are 45,540 places of work; ten years ago there were 28,135. If the whole church could be endued with the spirit of the Moravians, the task would be undertaken in a manner that would need no apologies. This little denomination of 30,000 Christians is to-day supporting over 400 missionaries, or one to every 68 members. The entire American church supports but one missionary to every 2,500 church members. The Moravians are giving $400,000 annually to support their mission churches, or $13 per caput for their membership. If all the churches did as well, the world would be evangelized in this generation. They have been the pioneers in most of the fields and have often turned over established stations to those who came after them. They have 100,000 gathered into their mission churches, and are pushing forward into unoccupied fields with true Apostolic zeal.

Here in the brilliantly illuminated civilization of a Christian land we are asking the men on the outposts, "Watchmen, what of the night?" Truly does the answer echo, "The morning cometh." Never since the dawn of civilization have the signs of its coming given such assurance. But figures do not adequately tell the story; they are but indexes to the larger volume of missionary accomplishment. Where thousands accept the definite evangel of the missioner, tens of thousands receive the benefits of his new truth and the better way of life. While a native church is being established, a whole nation is being leavened with a higher ideal and the old is giving way to the new. The missionary is the pioneer of a new epoch in the life of every people to whom he goes. In the West we are not all Christians, but we all live in Christian lands. So in the East, and in the savage lands, the missionary is bringing that social uplift that transforms custom and elevates whole nations and changes the face of the earth.

3. THE LEAVEN IN THE LUMP.

Christianity is taking the world "because it meets and supplies the deepest wants of men more perfectly than any other religion meets and supplies them," says Dr. Gladden. It is not claimed that Christ is the sole cause of progress, but that in his gospel and life are the most powerful factors that make for progress. John Fiske said that "religion is the largest and most ubiquitous fact connected with the existence of mankind upon the earth." "Pagan religion stopped the hand and neglected the heart," said Montesquiue. The Christian religion begins with the heart, and, placing there the motive power of action, sets the hand to every task that will redound to human welfare. Other systems may give ethical codes, but they bind them about the minds of men with a restricting literalism, while Christianity plants the seeds of principle in the hearts of men and leaves life to develop according to any variation that race, clime, or custom may demand. Judaism and Confucianism gave the Golden Rule negatively; they asked men to refrain from evil. But Christ gave it positively; he asked men to prosecute the doing of good. Between the two modes of action there is a continent of indifference. The one does no harm for self's sake; the other does good for other's sake.

Emerson said that the character of people was determined by their conception of God. Buddhism worships the perfected man. Gautauma taught that there was nothing better to worship. He spent his life thinking through the problems of suffering and death. He forsook wife and child to lead an ascetic life, and to find the way of escape from the miseries of existence. His disciples practice charity for merit's sake, but the world is not good and God is not interested in a perfected social relationship. The end of the best life is either absorption of one's personality into Nirvana, or complete oblivion. Self-annihilation is not a social ideal. The extinction of desire is the supreme moral end of life to the faithful Buddhist.

Confucius taught that men should "respect the gods, but let them alone." Confucianism really has no personal God. Its disciples leave the worship of "Shangte" to the emperor. Most of them accept the spirit worship of Taoism and make obiesence to the tablets of their ancestors. Man has a duty to fellow-man, but it does not hinge upon his conception of God, and therefore lacks the moral sanction that Christian theism gives. Brahmanism has many gods. It boasts of a pantheon of 330,000,000 divinities. Its great deities are anything but moral examples. They are really incarnations of human desires; in them is found the entire gamut of human passions. Salvation is not through fellow-help nor love of one's kind. Their best sacred book, the Bhagavad Gita, teaches that

50

even the evil person who worships correctly is deemed good. This illustrates the morals of the system. Mohammedanism teaches there is "one God and Mohammed is his prophet." It is not only monotheistic, it is iconoclastic. The future is fixed; law is supreme; none but Moslems can be saved. Mercy is not a tenet of Islamism. "After twelve centuries the Arabs are a nation of robbers," says Professor Marshall. It is no part of man to create a better order, God has fixed everything from the beginning.

None of these religions teach any such thing as a Kingdom of God. That which is the social inspiration and goal of Christianity is either denied or omitted by all of them. Their gods are either aloof, or non-existent, or implacable, or else they are interested only in a personal salvation. The world is either totally bad, is growing worse, or is a "wheel" upon which man is broken. It is never conceived of as a place into which "the heavens shall descend," and there "shall be a new heaven and a new earth." "One who has not examined the other religions can not know what Christianity really is," said Max Müller. Christianity is "the social hope of the nations," as Dr. Dennis demonstrates in his monumental work entitled, "Christian Missions and Social Progress."

If, as Fichte said, religion "seeks the realization of universal reason," may we not say that its end is the highest good of all? Benjamin Kidd, in his "Social Evolution," defines the scope of religion as being the subordination of the personal interests of the individual to the social organism, and says each type of civilization receives its characteristics from the ethical system implanted in it. According to his interpretation of history, not economics, nor politics, nor racial types, nor any other single thing determines the evolution of progress, but amid them all religion is the most powerful factor. It strikes deepest into human motives, and though it be inscrutable to those who profess it, it nevertheless furnishes the chief sanctions for action.

Christianity is neither a system of doctrine nor of morals, though it furnishes the world with both. Its dynamic is in a person. Christ said he was "the way, the truth, and the life," and "I came to bring life and bring it more abundantly." He asked the world to learn of him, but it was not in knowledge, but in doing that it was to find life. Christ exists to-day in millions of hearts, not merely as a philosopher or a lawgiver nor even as a saint, but as a friend and helper, the most vital reality in experience. No other religion offers the dynamic of such a personality. "Social efficiency rests upon qualities of character." If, as Kidd says, "the one essential" is supernatural sanction of some kind for acts and observances which have a social significance, then Christianity's secret as the greatest social leaven in the lump of the world is explained by the character of its founder and the mystery of his abiding presence in the hearts of his followers. His was "the mightiest heart that ever beat—stirred by the Spirit of God; how it wrought in his bosom," said Theodore Parker. In his life men find that ideal which the minds of the greatest have ever sought in vain in their visions. In his promises they discover principles of action that "decide questions we scarcely dare agitate as yet." In his love they discover the most indefinable mystery that even religion has to offer. Other religions have their martyrs, men who died rather than surrender their faith, but what other religion sends men gladly to a living martyrdom that they may give self for the sake of others? Here is the social power of Christ's religion, his "throne is a cross," his inspiration is that of human service, his way of life is through good to others. "The power of the love of Christ has been displayed alike in the most heroic pages of Christian martyrdom, in the most pathetic pages of Christian resignation, in the tenderest pages of Christian charity," says Lecky. "If the life and death of Socrates were those of a philosopher, the life and death of Jesus were those of a God," said Rousseau.

The reproach of Christ was the source of his power. "He emptied himself, taking the form of a servant." So his disciples were exhorted by Paul, in his letter to the Philippians, to be of the same mind, and in lowliness, each counting other better than himself, think of the things of others as their own. It has been the inner circle of the faithful that has given the world its Christian civilization. The virtues they display are those we turn to for the explanation of all that is best in our civilization. Christian sacrifice is not for personal escape of penalty, but for the help of the "least of these." If it be said that "salvation is character," it can, too, be said that sacrifice is service. The Emperor Julian reproached Christianity for its doctrine of the equality of man. By that doctrine it has overthrown despotisms and destroyed feudalisms and created democracies. Lucian ridiculed it for brother love and especially love of slaves, "whom the gods ignored as men of inferior nature." But that brother love has lifted up the fallen and made the very salt of society. Through it slavery has been overthrown and millions redeemed from bondage. By it the teaching of Plato and Aristotle that the masses can be but hewers of wood and drawers of water, and therefore have no place but to serve the elect of the race, has been supplanted by making of them citizens in their own right and by giving the government of nations to their will. Celsus satirized it for its message to the poor and weak and sinful. But Gibbon said, that while the empire deteriorated in luxury, a pure and humble religion gently insinuated itself into the minds of men, grew up in obscurity, derived new vigor from opposition, and finally planted its banner of the cross on the ruins of the capitol. The dispossessed are made the redeemed, the humble are exalted into greatness, the poor become rich in those things that do not destroy character. As egoism, privilege, and luxury ruin a people, Christianity saves through the implanting of unselfishness, charity, and humility.

"It was reserved for Christianity to present to the world an ideal character, which through all the changes of eighteen centuries has inspired the hearts of men with an impassioned love, has shown itself capable of acting upon all ages, nations, temperaments, conditions, has been not only the highest pattern of virtue but the strongest incentive to practice, and has exercised so deep an influence that it may be truly said that the simple record of three short years of active life has done more to regenerate and soften mankind than all the disquisitions of philosophers and all the exhortations of moralists," says Lecky, in his "History of European Morals."

It is this same religion that, in its purity and gentleness, is insinuating itself into the arrested life of archaic nations, planting itself in the unleavened mass of heathen races, bringing to them a light in learning, and giving them that mightiest of all civilizing agencies, the consecrated personalities of men devoted to their welfare. "Subtract the Christian personalities and the ideas that reigned in and lived through them, and you have but the struggle of brutal passions, of men savage through ambition and lust of power," says Dr. Fairbairn.

Civilization is awakening to the fact that "there is also a missionary interpretation of history." Carlyle believed that progress came through the leadership of "heroes" and by "hero worship." A more modern theory is that it comes through the leavening personalities and combined activities of groups of men devoted to a common idea. The missionary goes as the emissary of a new and better day. He alone of all the men who reside in foreign lands is there for an utterly unselfish purpose. He alone of all classes of men who mingle with alien peoples believes in their potentialities, and has supreme confidence that what has made him an enlightened being can make every other man the same. He has nothing to ask but a chance to be understood and an opportunity to apply his gospel. He is never defeated, for if he dies there are always ten to ask for his place. His sufferings

55

are turned into balms of blessing for the children of his tormentors, and, if he is martyred, his "blood becomes the seed of the church." He is the "pioneer in every reform, whether it be religious, social, or moral," said Tahil Ram Gunga Ram, a Hindu scholar. All are impressed by "the nobility of spirit, the simplicity of life, and the single-minded devotion to high aim," claimed for him by Sir Chas. A. Elliott, Lieut.-Governor of Bengal. He is a "worker together with God," and "fills up in his own body what lacks of the sufferings of Christ," that by his sacrifice he may communicate the sacrifice of Christ. There are many testimonies to his efficiency in the work he goes to do. Two will be given here. One is taken from the *Japanese Mail*, a secular paper, edited by non-Christians, and quoted by Dr. Dennis. "They lead the most exemplary lives; devote themselves to deeds of charity; place their educational and medical skill at the free disposal of the people, and exhibit in the midst of sharp suffering and diversity a spirit of patience and benevolence such as ought to enlist universal sympathy and respect." The other is from the words of Sir Harry H. Johnstone, British High Commissioner to East Central Africa, and a man who has spent many years in mission lands. He says, "They have done more good than armies, navies, and treaties have yet done."

4. TIME AND THE TIDES.

Customs change slowly. Nations and civilizations are not made in a day. The Kingdom of God cometh without observation. It is first the blade, then the ear, and then the full corn in the ear. Progress produces its cataclysms, but its great eras are not produced by cataclysms. The progress of Christian civilization is that of the leaven in the lump. There is much yet to be leavened. It is, indeed, one of the supreme obligations of the church to create social justice at home that she may the better deal with the social problems she is creating in the rejuvenation of the peoples of the earth. We are not yet purged of all our paganism; when we are the millennium will have come. Our confidence is in the comparison we can make with the social conditions that Christ found in the world, and those that the missionary finds where Christ is not known. What the missionary finds is a challenge to us to give what we have received in the faith that what has been done for us will, by the same power, be done for them.

The Roman historian, Tacitus, tells the story of our pagan ancestors in the forests of the Rhine. They had reached about the same status as had the American Indian found by the white man in this country. They were a barbarous folk, dressing in skins and dwelling in caves and in tents of hide. The men fought and followed the chase, and the women cultivated rude plots of ground. They were straight, ruddy of complexion, blonde haired, deep chested, and vigorous. They ate raw meat, and, in times of great victory, drank from the skulls of their vanquished foes. If they wanted a bird to eat, they selected a smooth stone from the brook, and, with the unerring aim of savage arms, skilled in all the arts of the chase, brought him down from his perch in the trees. If they wanted fish, they either trapped it with their hands or hooked

57

it with the breastbone of a small bird. If they ran across a bear they surrounded him, as the Africans do the hippopotami, and beat him to death with their clubs. The Prussians of North Germany and the Druids of England made human sacrifices, and it is probable that all the tribes north of the Alps did so until centuries after the beginning of the Christian era.

Culture failed to make Grecian civilization permanent. There lived at one time in Athens, then a city of less than ten thousand, no fewer than eighty-four men whose names are known until this day. Greek sculpture and Greek physic have never been surpassed, and Greek philosophy is still mediating the speculations of thinkers; but Greek civilization failed. It did not have the saving salt of social righteousness. Its democracy even was that of an aristocracy, while the masses were but servants of the elect. The famed Roman Republic went down upon the bar of patricianism. No civilization will endure if it sets itself to cultivate a privileged few. Its only surety of permanence is in the steady progress of its powers in creating a democracy. Roman power became the power of the select and privileged; social justice was not created; there was no equality of man and no enthusiasm for humanity. The emperor became the state. Stoic jurisprudence did much to evolve a technical justice, but it never recognized essential human equality; it never gave the slave human rights, and it never elevated woman to the plane of man before the law. The voice of the people never became the voice of God in imperial Rome.

Individual rights were suborned in favor of patrician privilege, and the state came to be administered for the benefit of the rulers. Material power became regnant—a sure sign of inner decay—and luxury brought dissipations that ruined the favored, while poverty brought weakness and immorality to the masses and thus undermined the foundations of society.

The social status of the society to which Paul took Christianity is indicated by the patriarchal state of the family. The father and husband was supreme. The wife was under "tutelage," *i. e.*, she was a minor before the law. If she brought a dowery, it passed from her control to that of her husband; her inheritance was only equal to that of one of the children. She had no legal rights over her offspring. She was an inferior being and her husband's rights were despotic. Children had no rights; they were the property of their father; he could expose them to death if not wanted at birth, or he could sell them to whomsoever he wished. The Lactrian columns in the midst of the city of Rome were the appointed place to which little ones could be brought and left to the tender mercies of the slaver, or of the man who wished a servant. Whosoever desired could take away the little body that parental obligation refused to consider, and for whom there was no parental love, unless perhaps it was that of a mother who dared not oppose her husband's determination to put it away. There were few mercies for the weak, the poverty-stricken starved without public relief, and the unfortunate bore their own burdens or died under them. Work was not respected. Labor had no dignity. It has little enough yet, but it is at least respectable, and has the right to its own body and to bargain for its own wage.

In the Roman Empire there were 60,000,000 slaves at the time of Christ. In Athens there were but 21,000 freemen when the population was 200,000. In Attica, the seat of culture, three out of every four were bondsmen. Plato made the majority of men slaves in his ideal republic. Aristotle condemned the majority to become hewers of wood and drawers of water, and had no faith that human nature could ever make them worthy of aught else. Cato allowed old and sick slaves to be disposed of as a burden. Cassius defended the law in a case where, according to law, 600 were executed because one had killed their master. Seneca says Pollio mutilated slaves in anger and fed their flesh to the fishes. Juvenal asked, "How can a slave be a man?" Ulpian speaks of "a slave or any other animal." Seneca said, "A slave has no home or religion." Stoical jurists ruled that they were property the same as animals. They could be attached for debt, their testimony was admissible only under torture, and marriage was never legalized for them. Their first gleam of hope came when Constantine's code began to implant the rudiments of the Christian ideals of humanity.

Paganism is egoistic, proud, and selfish. It seeks every one his own and might makes right. Christianity is altruistic and implants a fundamental respect for the things of the other man. Harnack says it was the moral power of Christianity that maintained it during the early centuries of persecution and finally carried the world for it. Greece and Rome were starkly individualistic. The church became popular and bargained with paganism. The pure faith was adulterated with heathen custom, and for a thousand years Christianity was shorn of her pristine moral power; but she never lost it, and during even the "Dark Ages" the leaven was working. Whatever the custom, it will be found that there was a protest somewhere among the prophetic souls who had not lost the vision, and that their light was as a pillar by night, guiding the courses of history.

Ulfilas crossed the Alps with the gospel in the year 344 A. D. He had been captured in one of the northern raids of the Emperor of the Eastern Empire and his ruddy vigor, fighting powers, and handsome countenance won him imperial favor. He was educated and was offered a place at the court, but he had attended the churches in Constantinople and learned the gospel of peace, and he longed to herald its message to his barbarous countrymen. He left court and civilization behind him and made his way alone to native land, with the sacred Scriptures as his choicest weapon. He translated the Bible into his native Gothic tongue, after having reduced it to writing. A single illuminated copy of his translation is yet held as an invaluable heirloom of Western civilization, and is preserved in the University of Upsala, in Sweden. In it our pagan forbears found the chart that led them into civilization. They were not transformed in a day; it took a thousand years to redeem them, and even then they had only purged out the grosser habits of barbarism; and it has taken another half millennium to bring the refinements of our modern life. It is the law of the leaven.

In the year 208 A. D., Tertullian wrote that "places in Britain not yet visited by the Roman are subject to Christ." In 314, British delegates are found at the Council of Arles. St. Patrick's work in Ireland was done during the first half of the fifth century. It was a century later before the gospel really obtained a hold in Scotland, through the work of Columba. Not until the year 700 A. D. could the British Isles be called in any sense Christian; it had taken five hundred years to make them so. Ireland became a missionary recruiting ground and "the greenest spot in Christendom." From her training schools and evangelical activities flowed out beneficent streams of missionary activity to Friesland and Germany. Willibrord pioneered on the mouth of the Rhine in the year 690 A. D. The Prussians were still killing their deformed children and their aged, and burying wives and slaves with their deceased lords. The Saxons were still sea-rovers and pirates. So savage were the North Germans, that for two centuries, between the years 1000 and 1200 A. D., none dared go to them. It was not until 1209 that a missionary, named Christian, succeeded in obtaining residence among them, and it was a thousand years from the days of Ulfilas before the gospel was recognized over all Western Europe. The hardy Norsemen were among the rudest and wildest of the Teutons. Willibrord went to them at the close of the seventh century, but was repulsed, and it was not until the year 827 A. D. that Ansgar began the work that finally prevailed. It took two hundred years to

A *Native Church in the Marshall Islands, South Pacific Seas.
Illustrating native carving and building under missionary
instruction.*

O *fficers of a Native Church in Marshall Islands. These
people were naked cannibals a generation ago.*

make Denmark Christian, and the island of Borneholm did not surrender until 1060. Sweden held out for another one hundred years, and Lapland did not yield until late in the thirteenth century.

If it took a thousand years to convert modern Europe, shall we not marvel at the progress made in a single century in an arrested civilization like that of China, or in that of a century and a half in an ancient and debilitated nation like India, or in the half century's attainments in proud Japan? These nations have the conservatism that comes with ancient custom and a static half-civilization. Christianity comes to them with the impact of its Western attainments; it is borne on the wings of inventions, and brings a world of progress that commends its message in a thousand ways. It has obtained a vast momentum in the world, and by that law it will overcome more quickly in the East than it did in the West. It is estimated that there were 50,000 Christians at the end of the first century. At the end of the first century of Protestant Missions in China there are 175,000 communicants, and at the end of the first half-century in Japan, much talked of as one of the fields of slow returns, there are more than 70,000 church members. Facts demonstrate where theories only contend. Christian missions bring the undeniable success of a new and better society, and challenge interest through the offer of a better way. In times of change men breathe ideals as atmosphere, and the masses adopt them without stopping to debate them. Thus there is a mighty evangelism in custom, and the Kingdom of God comes in ways that figures can not register.

Time and the tides of progress make for a new era, new ideas create new forms, and whole peoples are lifted nearer unto the Kingdom that Christ came to establish in the earth.

5. THE MAN AND THE IDEA.

The Duke of Argyle said that when you planted an incompatible idea down alongside a false belief, a superstitious practice, or a cruel custom, there was bound to be a revolution. The missionary is a man with an idea. And he not only possesses the idea, it possesses him, it is incarnate in him, he becomes the idea in action. That idea is one that brings a sublime faith in the possibility of man; it fills him with an optimistic outlook on the world; it is backed by unshrinking confidence in the potentiality of his own life, weak as it may be, because he feels God is in it; it gives him a vision and he lives for it, though never expecting to live to see it, for he is strangely unselfish of that which moves most men to action and enjoys giving his life for others. His idea is that the good news of Christ is able to save unto the uttermost. But he does not expect that idea to work by itself. Christianity is never impersonal. When Peter confessed the Lordship of Jesus, the Master told him that it was upon such confessions he would build his church. The Church of Christ was to be builded out of men who accepted his Lordship and undertook to live his kind of life. Paul told certain of his converts that they were his "epistles, known and read of all men." The missionary not only takes the gospel, he is the gospel, and the testimony from the foreign field is universal

64

that the mightiest factor in the winning of the pagan to Christ is the life and love of the missioner. "The mightiest civilizing persons are Christian men," said Dr. Fairbairn. He goes, not to confer blessings but to implant them, and when he gets them truly implanted into the hearts of his hearers they in turn become incarnations of the idea and carry it on to others.

Henry Van Dyke tells a little legend of how Jesus was condoled with when he reached Paradise because his project of saving the world had so tragically failed through his life being taken away. He replied, in surprise, that there had been no failure, for Peter and John and all the disciples would tell it to others, and these in turn to others, and so as each heard and accepted he would tell it to others, until at last the whole world shall have heard it and believed, and the Kingdom of God will have come. Darwin said, "The lesson of the missionary is that of an enchanter's wand." He was atheistic so far as the claims of theology were concerned, but in islands off the coast of Patagonia he had seen the transformation wrought by the missionary, and his faith in their power to make mightily for the evolution of mankind was so great that he sent a missionary contribution thereafter every year of his life. What was true of Darwin is true in this day, both at home and abroad. The journalistic interest in missions, which has so rapidly arisen in the past few years, is because men of the world have seen the forces for civilization laid by the missionary and noted that the results are fairly dramatic in their surprises. The awakening of statesmen

5   65

has not been a theological but a sociological awakening, and they advocate missions because of their contribution to human progress. In the foreign fields themselves the leaders of the nations which are adjusting themselves to the world order of affairs do not hesitate to give the missionary his just assessment as a contributor to their new national life. They contribute to his schools and hospitals and read his literature; they invite him into their councils and send their sons to him that he may prepare them to take part in the new order of things; they testify that he brought the idea to them and that his life has commended it to all who have understood.

The missionary is thus the pioneer of social progress in the non-progressive and barbarious nations. He alone goes without a selfish interest. He alone seeks to understand the people to whom he has gone, and to confer benefits instead of seeking them. He alone does not despise them, but gives them his fullest confidence and advocates their cause even though they underestimate his motives, or even if they so fail to understand him as to traduce him and martyr him. Greatest of all, he communicates his spirit to his converts and they become willing sacrifices upon the altar of the old order that the new may come. The history of every great missionary success is written in the sweat and blood of the native converts. If they have not given their lives in blood and flame, as in the martyrdoms of Uganda, Madagascar, and China, they have given them in living sacrifices for the sake of their neighbors whom the gospel taught them to love. Their teacher incarnates in them his own

Christ-like faith in men. In Korea the native elders of many churches will not accept an inquirer for baptism until he has brought another inquirer to be taught. In Samoa, Robert Louis Stevenson, who had met most of the great of earth in his time, said of one of the native missioners, that he was the finest specimen of Christian manhood he had ever looked upon. James Chalmers wrought for years with the native missioners of the South Seas, and boldly compared them with the choicest and most heroic spirits of history. In China to-day young men are turning from lucrative governmental positions to teach their fellows the riches of the knowledge of Christ. The missionary gives the people a vision and they do not perish, but are made alive with new life. He multiplies his number by scores and finally by hundreds and thousands, and these become the leaven of the nation. Their numbers are no criterion to their value in the life of the people. Their influence is out of all proportion to their power. Upon their backs, as upon that of Atlas, a world is lifted into new being.

It was an apothegm of ancient paganism that "a man is a wolf to a man he does not know." The missionary turns men from the conquest of one another to that of self and of nature and its hidden powers. He teaches the Brotherhood of Man, and puts faith in the place of the old and paralyzing suspicion that characterizes heathenism. He demonstrates that it is more heroic to die for a cause yourself than it is to kill another in behalf of a cause. His way of progress is by means of service rather than by the way of material gain. He brings material gain as one of the

67

inevitable consequences of civilization, and a new conception of toil as more honorable than idleness, and implants the revolutionary idea that every individual has an inalienable right to his own life and the fruits thereof, but he does not bring a materialistic conception of progress, nor seek to confer a higher life through the worship of mammon. With Edward Everett Hale he believes that "progress is always spiritual," and so seeks to found the fundamentals of it in the moral life of a people that the flood and ebb tides of worldly acquisition will never be able to sweep them off its firm foundations.

The religion he takes is unlike all others in that it is not racial or nationalistic. It does not rely upon mass movements for its conquests, nor seek to gain peoples through battles, or by law. Charlemagne sought to convert the Saxons to his half-learned Christianity by a military crusade. He had to repeat the military invasion several times, but found that they were as pagan as ever. A wise bishop of the church advised him to try the more Christly method of persuasion and benevolence, and they were won. Vladimir accepted Christianity as a matter of state and sent priests with soldiers to baptize his subjects. They had the choice of baptism or death and chose the former, and Russia is unto this day half pagan; it has a form of religion without the substance thereof. Christianity makes its appeal to the individual. Jesus frankly sought out men. He refused to lead a nationalistic movement and spent much of his time with single individuals. His conquest of the earth must proceed by the process of winning single individuals. But these individuals are never to be individualistic. They become social factors in just the measure that they become his men. None of them lives unto himself, but counts the things of others as his own. The individual is the beginning of the conquest, but society is the end; he is the factor through whom the gospel works for the upbuilding of the Kingdom of God, but he is never apart from the whole of humanity, nor is his obligation ever discharged until the whole world is redeemed, and redeemed in all its ways. A native Hindu has said, in commending Christianity, "The best way to raise the individual is to raise the society of which he is a member."

The missionary goes to his task with a divine patience. He looks upon himself as a "worker together with God," and he is willing to sow and nurture while a Divine Providence brings in the increase. Livingstone and Gordon knew Africa, and felt its woes as did no other living men, but they did not fret over it. They knew that the processes of a universe are slow and they were willing to wait, content only if they had done their part. The missionary idea is optimistic. It is surcharged with the faith that all things are possible. History testifies eloquently to its force, even when it has been borne in earthen vessels. It comes not with theories or speculations or ologies, but with life itself. Stanley believed that if all the rest of the world were suddenly bereft of Christianity, there was enough vigor and understanding of the simple and essential things of it in the native Uganda church to spread it over the world again.

It has been a man with an idea that has inaugurated

every reform and marked the beginning of every new epoch. The idea of Jesus that every man could be saved, and that it was possible to create a perfect moral order of society through fealty to the things desired by the Heavenly Father, is the most potential that was ever loosed in the minds of men. It is the missionary idea, and with it the missioner goes to his task, "becoming all things to all men, if by any means he may win some." He makes commerce and railroads and telegraphs and schoolhouses and governments his handmaidens, but the thing he does is to create a new Brotherhood of Man in the name of him who was a friend to every man.

CHAPTER II

The Home: The Corner-Stone of Civilization

1. House or Home.

Christianity offers the world the ideal of a home. Paganism has no term for home. The abiding places of men are simply houses. Where there is no mutual refinement or respect between husband and wife there can be no true home. Heathenism demands that the wife regard the husband with an attitude of worship, while he may look upon her with total disrespect. In him she is to find her salvation. Dr. W. A. P. Martin says he saw three thousand women praying in a temple in China, and their petition was that they might be reborn men. Hinduism and Buddhism alike teach that her only hope is to serve him faithfully, that she may be saved with him and serve him forever. Thus she has willingly immolated herself on his grave and received praise for her devotion, for her husband was her god.

The Koran is a man's Bible. Woman had greater respect in Arabia before Mohammed than she has under his teachings. To satisfy his desire for many wives the rule of polygamy was made. He limited his followers to four wives each, but took many more himself, and allowed concubinage. He sanctified polygamy, slavery, and divorce, and made them all man's prerogative, while woman became the victim of each one. Consequently there is no home in Islam. The harem is a house where the wives, concubines, and slaves of the wealthy Moslem are kept. It knows nothing of love unless it be the passing favor of the lord for some pretty young inmate of his establishment. It is a place of jealousy, intrigue, and suspicion. Mrs. Isabella Bird Bishop says she was approached scores of times with the request for poison to put an end to the life of the favorite or her child. She describes the pleasures of the harem as being disgusting, and the language of common conversation unfit for refined ears.

What is true of the harem is true of all polygamous homes. They are simply houses where the family live and are sheltered and fed, but they have none of the sanctity of a real home, nor can they have, for two wives can not dwell together in harmony—it is not nature's design. Polygamy implies the subjection of woman and the lordship of man, and thus destroys that equality without which a home can not be founded. There is a Hindu proverb which says, "The cow is sanctified, but woman is depraved." The masses of people do not accept that proverb literally, for there is much affection between husbands and wives, and especially do sons reverence their mothers as far as it is possible for a "superior" being to reverence an "inferior." But the ideals of heathenism are all against the wife and mother because she is a woman. Christianity offers no loftier sentiment than that for mother. Its ideals exalt woman's function and thus exalt the home and make it what De Tocqueville called it—"The cornerstone of the nation."

The family meal is the altar of the Christian home. There reverence and gratitude are paid the Creator, and the sacrament of family communion is kept. The bonds of family affection and mutuality are hallowed with converse over topics of common interest, and all minds and hearts are made one as they partake of the food that is provided by the co-operation of all its members. The pagan family does not have the common meal. In Africa and other savage lands the woman eats alone and after her lord has departed. In more cultured pagan lands she serves him and partakes of what is left. Among some barbarous peoples she is not allowed to eat of the same kind of food that he does. Even in Japan it is not good form for the ladies of the house to eat with the husband and guests. The rule in pagan households is for the sexes to eat separately. The female members of the house are the servants of the male members.

Modesty is the means in which society clothes itself for the protection of the finer sentiments, and the practice of it is the line of demarcation between the lower and higher forms of social life. It begins in the home and in the mutual regard its members possess for one another. It is the safeguard thrown about young people to guarantee purity of manners and the sanctity of virtue in their commingling. It is wholesome when it is unconsciously practiced, but becomes a means of unholiness when it is not natural and worn with grace. Christianity cultivates a natural modesty. It clothes womankind with refinement of manners

73

and gives her the freedom of friendship and the fellowship of innocence. Paganism suspects womankind. It regards her as a snare rather than a grace, and a danger instead of an inspiration. It allows no courtship because it has no confidence in virtue. The right to choose a life companion is denied youth. The contract is made by parents or guardians, and there is usually a money consideration involved. The exchange of money implies the relationship of servant where the groom pays for it, or that girls are a burden to be disposed of where the father of the bride pays it. In savagery girls are sold as slaves and treated as such. A man's wealth and social position are determined by the number of wives or female slaves he possesses. In India girls are a burden because they must be married with a dowery, *i. e.*, some man must be paid for taking them. In both cases there is a sensual idea of woman's position. In the zenana she is kept in seclusion because she is not trusted. The purdah is the result of an age-long attitude of suspicion toward womankind. The Moslem either confines his wife in the harem or compels her to wear a veil in public. In either case he advertises his distrust of her and breaks down that sense of unconscious modesty that makes womankind the symbol of all that is purest and best to the Christian mind. Her seclusion, and the walls of distrust built around her by heathenism, deprive her of confidence and destroys her integrity.

It is a Christian proverb that no house is large enough for two families. Every home has its holy of holies, into which none may come but its own im-

mediate members. The intimate bonds of the home
are those of closest relationship, and to destroy the
inner confidences with the encroachment of even be-
loved friends or other relatives is to weaken the home
bonds themselves. Christianity says a man shall
leave his father and mother and cleave unto his wife,
and they twain shall be one flesh. The patriarchal
household makes this close attachment impossible.
In India and China as many as forty are found under
one patriarchal roof. Sons bring their wives to the
parental roof-tree, and all are subject to the father so
long as he lives. The daughter-in-law must obey
her husband's mother, and is often the subject of
tyranny. There is a common treasury and the mother
provides the common pantry. Delinquent members
of the family come to be provided for, and there is no
inspiration for the various individuals to cultivate
thrift. Idleness begets idleness, and all are pulled
down toward the level of the least worthy of the household. The house is the scene of quarreling between
the various wives and families, and envy, distrust,
and jealousy run riot. An imperious old woman can
make life an inferno for every daughter-in-law, and
sons are set at strife in defense of their families, or
husbands and wives at variance through hatred of the
women for one another. The intimate confidences
are lost to the children. They have no sense of family
life as they have in a Christian home, and are used
to bickering and strife, and learn to be selfish instead
of mutually helpful. There is much unrest with this
manner of life in India wherever the better way of
independent homes is seen through the coming of

Western ways, but the orthodox sentiment is yet so strong that when the Madras legislature passed a law legalizing the right of every man to his independent earnings, riot was threatened and the law repealed.

The permanence of the home depends upon the sanctity of the marriage relation. The divorce evil is one that demands attention in our Christian lands, but if it is menacing here what shall we say of it in pagan lands, where there is almost no constraint? In civilized Japan every sixth marriage is dissolved; a few years ago it was every third one. Japan now has a law that makes divorce a matter of court decree, but it still allows the bond to be dissolved by mutual agreement, and, as a matter of fact, the larger number are thus dissolved. China allows seven causes for divorce, among which is talkativeness. Nearly all pagan lands allow a woman to be put away if she is childless, and most of them give the husband practically the sole right of divorce. Mohammedanism gives the husband the sole right; the common practice is to have one wife at a time, but to have many in the course of a lifetime. Short time marriages are common in Arabia and Turkey. One resident in Arabia says he scarcely knows of a man of thirty that has not been married to from two to five women. Where woman is not on a plane of equality with man he will not greatly respect her rights. If he regards her as having no soul, or as an inferior order of being, he will not be sensitive to her feelings. Where she is his servant and pawn, he ceases to think of her as one having rights, and so regards only his own selfish privileges and acts accordingly.

76

THE HOME

The mission church insists strongly on the sanctity of the home, and makes regard for it a condition of membership. If a man has two or more wives he must put away all but one. This is a stumbling-block to many and a hardship to some, but it is the lesser of all the evils involved, for without a monogamous home there can be no permanent Christianity and no civilization worth the having. "A nation will not be better than its homes," says Shailer Mathews. Jesus made much of the home in his teachings, and used it as type and symbol in the profoundest things of his discourses. It is the cornerstone of civilization. From it flows all other virtues, and the safety of the home is the guarantee of progress. So the missionary refuses to recognize concubinage and polygamy and casual divorce. The young Korean and Chinese churches expel members who take concubines. There are no excuses or relenting, though it is a native proverb that "A man marries his wife, but loves his concubine." A native Chinese Christian tells blushingly of how embarrassed he felt when he determined to walk with his wife upon the street, and of how such custom as the church taught him brought respect, and finally true affection for the woman to whom his parents had married him without his having seen her before the wedding day. In Japan the Christian custom is fast taking hold of the family relationship, and husbands and wives may be seen in public and at the table together. When the present Mikado proclaimed the constitutional régime he rode in public procession with his wife, and thus recognized a new attitude toward women; but he celebrated the twenty-fifth anniversary

77

of his accession to the throne by taking another concubine, and his heir is the son of one of these secondary wives. The crown prince, however, has only one wife and treats her with all the respect of Christian custom.

The missionary makes a specialty of girls' schools. In India but one woman in every 170 can read. The missionary aims to teach every girl that comes into the church to read, and one-third of all the pupils in mission schools are girls. In Syria, Turkey, and Egypt especially are schools for girls thriving. The modern youth seek them for wives and they are honored. Their homes are models of cleanliness, as compared with the old type, and they preserve their womanly independence; refinement and reticence take the place of the old vulgarities, and the Christian home can be selected immediately from among those not yet redeemed by the higher ideals. Heathenism does not govern with a rational discipline, as indeed ignorance never does, but beats when angry and coddles when in good humor. The Christian home brings a higher type of intelligence and a more normal discipline for children, and above all, it brings a like regard for boys and girls. When plagues break out the Christian cottage is more nearly immune, because sanitation has been taught there and thus life is better preserved. In Samoa the missionaries established a school for the instruction of young married couples in the art of home-making. Marriage is made a matter of affection and not of barter, and the young lady is given, first, the right to womanhood before being compelled to enter domestic relation, and, second, the right to her own will in the choice of a husband. If custom

78

demands that she be not courted, as is allowed in Christianized lands, she can at least see the lad who is proposed for her and exercise the right of veto.

2. THE INDEX OF PROGRESS.

The place accorded woman in a society is an index of its state of progress. If no nation can endure half slave and half free, no society can progress half servant and half master. The laws of a state are a record of its customs; the maxims of its sages and wise men are records of its ideals. With these two records before us we have an understanding of the place accorded woman by the ancients.

In the Roman world woman was a ward of her husband. She was never his equal before the law but was under "tutelage," *i. e.*, under his protection and treated as a minor. In Greece not even her father could legally will her an estate in her own right. She had no freedom to go abroad before her marriage, but was kept in seclusion until she could go in her husband's right. Aristotle gave her a place between that of a freeman and a slave, and Plato said her place and honor consisted in keeping the house and obeying her husband. That great philosopher suggested a community of wives and that none should know which were her own children, in order that they might be made better citizens of the state; not a high tribute to motherhood to say the least. Pericles thought her most highly honored when no one spoke of her; as if the very mention of her was an immodesty. In Greece, as in Rome, she was a minor before the law and was treated as were her own children.

In both Greece and Rome the husband had the legal power of life and death over his wife and children. The patriarchal forms inhered in the legislation of these governments. Upon marriage, any property she possessed passed into the absolute control of her husband. She could make no legal bargain after marriage, but must act through her husband. To mingle with freemen in public and listen to the lectures of the philosophers of olden Greece, or to obtain education for herself and have part in the learned professions, she was compelled to accept the position of an unchaste woman. Aspasia and others of the noted women of ancient learning accepted this portion that they might break the barriers that stood between womankind and a life of learning. The law expressed the position which she held in common judgment, though law usually follows the progress of custom, and she was often accorded privileges before the law recognized them. Augustus legalized concubinage, and in all social life the trend of imperial Rome was downward from the more severe codes of the republic. She was distrusted by the sages, and their ideas offered no hope of a better position to her. Plato spoke of her as "that part of the race which is by nature prone to secrecy and stealth." Seneca thought most women to be "cruel and incontinent in their desires." Cato declared "all women were plaguey and proud," and expelled Manilius from the Senate "because he had kissed his wife in the daytime and in the presence of his daughter."

So severe was the law that custom ran counter to it and there grew up a form of "free marriage" in

Rome. It gave woman more freedom, but did it at the cost of her morals and her influence. Under it she could hold her own property and retain membership in her father's family, but the result was short-time marriages and every form of marital looseness. She could divorce her husband, and Seneca said, "There are women who count their years, not by the number of consuls, but by the number of their husbands." Gibbon says that "passion, interest, caprice, suggested daily motives for the dissolution of marriages." She had her choice between respectability under repression of her individuality, or freedom at the expense of her virtue. In neither case was she in a position of equality with her brother.

Our Teutonic ancestors, according to Tacitus, purchased their wives and held right of life and death over them by law, but held them in much higher esteem than did the Romans. She shared his camp and wilderness life and with him bore the burdens of war and the chase. Anglo-Saxon wives were known to have immolated themselves on their husband's grave. Polygamy was not unknown, but one husband, one wife, was the rule, and infidelity on the part of the wife was terribly punished at the husband's discretion. Her virtues were prized and she could inherit property from her father, though her husband alone could sell and manage her estate. She was under tutelage because she could not fight, but her position was a vast improvement over that of the luxurious South. Says Tacitus, "They carry on their affairs, fenced about with chastity, corrupted by no enticements of spectacles, by no excitements of convivial feasts."

When these barbarians made conquest of Rome, they were horrified by the state of life they found, but fortunately Christianity had come with its redemptive social power and showed them the promise of better manners.

In the accounts of the life of Christ, and in the history of the Apostolic church, woman is accorded honor and esteem. Marriage vows were strict and the bond was one of equality. Through the infant church there grew up in the midst of ancient society the norm of a better social and family life, that in the course of time elevated woman to a position of universal honor and issued in the chivalric devotion of the middle ages. Formerly her weakness had made her the object of subjection, but it now came to make her the object of protection. Chivalry tended to make her but an ornament and to set her aside from the courses of virile life, but, once her position was redeemed from that of tutelage, she claimed her intellectual rights. The early church recognized her as an office-bearer and as the chief ministrant of charity. If it denied her the privilege of public discourse, it was only to save her from the criticism of an age that conceived of all public women as of doubtful character, and to the more securely fix respect for her in the public mind.

Constantine's laws first adopted Christian principles in any form into the Roman code. He did not go far in his inculcation of them, but he recognized them. He gave woman equal civil rights with man, and abolished concubinage and forbade any woman remarrying who had divorced her first husband without good cause. The later and more Christian code of Justinian abolished the absolute power of the husband, gave the wife legal rights to movable property, allowed her to become the legal tutor of her children, and began to make her the mother that modern law proclaims her to be. In the middle ages the church was paganized by the world to such an extent that the Christian ideal made slow progress, but the voice of the church councils was generally in favor of the larger rights of womankind. Canon law, i. e., the law of the church, was more progressive in regard to women, children, and slaves than were the laws of the kings. The Christian kings from the days of Ethelbert of Kent and of Charlemagne led in the recognition of woman's growing rights, and especially sought to redeem her from purchase and insure her a dowery. Charlemagne took severe measures to repress divorce and declared he made the laws in recognition of the principles of Christianity. She was finally allowed to appear in court in her own behalf, and at last, in the thirteenth century, France declared her no longer under "tutelage." The old Germanic idea of force as the source of authority began to give way to the more benign precepts of Christianity, and the theory of innate human rights began to take its place.

The story of civilization is the story of woman's progress. No society can advance beyond the ideals it holds of motherhood. Christianity has abolished bridal purchase and has elevated woman from legal tutelage to the position of a freeman before the law; it has made marriage a bond of the soul, and the wife a companion of her husband instead of his servant;

it gave the mother the right of guardianship over her children, reserved to her the privilege of giving her own hand in wedlock, and put her on an equality with her spouse in the obtaining of divorce. The religion of Jesus has ever championed the cause of the oppressed. It knows neither male nor female, neither bond nor free. In all its conquests it has plead the cause of woman and rapidly placed her upon a higher plane in society. No wonder the old pagan philosopher cried, "What women these Christians have!" She has ever held honorable place in the Christian church, and her virtues are the noblest our religion celebrates. "It is a fact significant for the past, prophetic for the future, that even as Dante measured his successive ascents in Paradise, not by immediate consciousness of movement, but by seeing an ever lovelier beauty in the face of Beatrice, so the race now counts the gradual steps of its spiritual progress, out of the ancient heavy glooms, toward the glory of the Christian millennium, not by mechanisms, not by cities, but by the ever new grace and force exhibited by the woman who was for ages either the decorated toy of man, or his despised and abject drudge," said the eloquent Dr. Stors.

3. Man Everything, Woman Nothing.

"The theory of heathenism is that man is everything and woman nothing," says one of the older missionaries to China. What was true of the world to which Christ came is true of the world to which his missionaries go to-day. The late Shah of Persia had eight hundred wives. The Emperor of China must have a royal household of women, and the higher officiary follow his example. The Sultan of Turkey takes slave girls only into his harem, and they are freed only upon the birth of sons. The late Sultan was known to have killed one of his slave wives with his own hand. The Mikado of Japan keeps concubines and the King of Siam is a polygamist. African chieftains count their wealth by the number of female slaves, and in all savagery woman is property to be inherited, purchased, and sold as material goods, or animals. In more cultured pagan lands she is at the disposal of her father in marriage, and man's powers border upon, if indeed they do not become, that of a slave owner. In China, Siam, and India monogamy is the rule among the masses, but concubinage is allowed to all who can afford it, and divorce is in the husband's hands. To say there are no happy women in paganism would be gross error, but the average of happiness and the possibilities of living any adequate life are far below the average of Christendom. Indeed, it may be said that the masses of heathen women are content with their lot, but it is because they know nothing else, and it is Christianity's part to arouse a discontent wherever humanity is not living up to its highest possibilities. If one desires womankind to be demure and ornamental and to act the part of a beautiful toy, he could not do better than to go to old Japan, where her subservience and ingrained modesty make her petit and winsome and obedient. If he wishes her to be subservient, obedient, industrious, and dutiful, let him go to China where she makes her husband her lord and lives for the sake of her sons. But if he wishes her to possess individuality, spirit, independence, and a mind of her own, he will go to no pagan land, but to those lands where Christianity has had the freest sway and she has come into that natural inheritance the Creator designed for all his children.

The proverbs and sayings of the sages are the same in modern pagan lands that they were in the ancient. In India the Laws of Manu proclaimed that "A woman is never fit for independence." They provided that she be dependent on her father until she had a husband, and upon her sons if her husband was deceased; if she had no father or sons, then upon her husband's nearest male relative, and if no male relative, then upon the sovereign. A reflection of this is found in medieval times by the Christian kings making the widow their special ward; but they made her such that they might provide her protection, while in heathenism she is made a pawn by those who are thus made her guardians. In India widowhood means disgrace. She must take off her jewels, shave her head, put on coarse garments, eat but once each day, attend no festivity, nor mingle with the crowd, for her presence is a curse; her husband is dead and she has no one to honor or live for, and, by the ideals of woman's place, should have died with him. She belongs to her husband for eternity and may not remarry, for her hope is in faithfulness to his memory; but if she had died first, her husband could remarry as often as he chose. She is preyed upon by wicked men, made a slave to her deceased husband's family, or sent home to be counted a burden in her father's household. In India there are to-day 25,000,000 of these poor, abject creatures of harsh misfortune, 115,000 of them under ten years of age, and none to pity aside from those whose hearts have been touched by the compassion of him who so often relieved the widow's distress, and made it the cardinal practice of his religion to visit her and her children in their distress.

"Man," said Confucius, "is the representative of Heaven and supreme over all things. Woman yields obedience to the instructions of man and helps to carry out his principles. She may take no step on her own notion and may come to no conclusion on her own deliberation." Like Manu, he prescribed that she must be obedient to her father, husband, or sons. He said the duties of the house were her sole business, and that "beyond the threshold of apartments she should not be known for evil or for good." The character that spells her name is closely akin to those that stand for strife and for disorderly conduct. Confucius' teachings regarding her individual rights were much like those of Plato. The Greater Learning said that "the only qualities that befit a woman are gentle obedience, chastity, mercy, quietness." Chinese women have excellent personal qualities, but are denied the rights of personality. She is married to whomsoever her parents choose and usually not allowed to see her betrothed until the wedding day. If she knows who he is it is immodest for her to speak to him or recognize him upon meeting. After marriage her husband may act without much reference to her feelings if he is so disposed. Very often he is kindly and treats her with regard, but it is not demanded of him by society. Her father may sell her if he chooses, and, in times of distress, does so without let or hindrance. She thinks of herself as an inferior being and knows nothing but the part of humiliation. If a Buddhist, she prays to be reborn a man that she may be saved, for none but men will be saved. As in all pagan lands, the philosophers look upon her as a necessary evil, and the masses make her a drudge. But in drudgery is her larger spiritual freedom. If she has to work she can not be confined to the house and her feet must not be bound. She is ignorant and apathetic toward the larger things of life and could not be expected to be aught but a gossip, a creature of intrigue, and quarrelsome. In savage lands she is frankly a slave. A man's wealth is measured by the number of his wives, *i. e.*, the number of his female slaves. She is the slave class because she is the drudge, while men are warriors and hunters. When protest was made to an African whose wife was carrying him over a stream on her back, he asked with all guilelessness, "If my wife should not carry me over, whose should?"

In pagan lands few women are ever allowed to claim the privileges of youth. They are married at tender age and burdened with the position of servant to their husband's mother and with the duties of motherhood. In China the term "slave-girl" is the one often applied to a bride, and she is married between the ages of seventeen and twenty. Her position is better there than in more southern Asiatic lands or in any of the savage lands. In India the Brahmanic law is that she must be married before twelve years of age, and one-half of all are wedded between the ages of ten and fourteen. The contempt of society is mightier than the law of the land, and not to be wedded before that age is to be disgraced. One girl child out of every eight is married between the ages of five and nine, and there are at least a quarter of a million who are betrothed in their cradles, or before the age of five years. In Moslem lands they are married before fourteen, and in Siam before twelve, or at thirteen she is sold as a serf to the highest bidder. In all these places spinsterhood is a disgrace not to be condoned, and if a girl can not be a wife she must be a slave. In Japan her father has a chattle right over her and may pawn her into disgrace as a pledge for money borrowed, or to pay a debt. Her only recompense is that the life into which she is thus bartered does not disgrace her for the conjugal relationship, and she may be married out of it in the course of time. This fact alone argues powerfully for the low plane of her position, as well as for the low order of morals in a nation.

Being an inferior person, it is not considered that she needs education. In China only one out of every two or three thousand can read and write. In India only six out of every thousand can do so, and the English Government provides a public school system. In Japan she is now being taught in the public schools and shows herself the equal of her brothers, as she ever has when allowed equal intellectual opportunities. Chinese girls find a wide open door and a crying need for their talents in medicine, and Japanese women are entering the teaching and nursing professions, after the manner of American and English young ladies. In India, where her ignorance is most abject and where it was said that you had as well put a razor in a monkey's hand as to give woman an education, she has furnished poets, novelists, teachers, and other leaders, especially in works of benevolence. Pandita Ramabai was widowed in early life, but she was in fortunate position, and coming to America interested Christian people in her design to found a home for her country's child widows. She began in 1889 with two, and now has over two thousand under her care in her community at Poona. Dr. W. A. P. Martin says the minds of these women are not dull, and that they are stupid only because untaught; that the girls of China are among the brightest of pupils and always possess the best morals. They have been reared in twilight, and when brought out into the sunlight of instruction they blossom with beauty. The untaught women of paganism become the chief conservers of the old ways, because they are immersed in superstition and are conservative through ignorance. To debase a mind is to make it its own worst enemy and to destroy within it all power of initiative. Women are the slowest to accept Christianity because they are most difficult of access, and because of the temperament acquired through subjection and superstitions. It is not to be thought that she has no influence. The very devotion in which she serves her lord gives her a vast influence over him. She has the care of her sons during their plastic early period of life, and as the only honor she receives is that of mother, she never loses a sort of dominance over them.

To the native mind it looks like social anarchy to

so radically change the position of woman and to so reorder all conceptions of the home as Christianity proposes. Most of the household acts of pagan life are radically connected with religion, and the superstitious mind can see nothing but religious disruption in the change. In China the worship of ancestors is a household act and woman can not perform it; she must provide sons or her husband and his ancestors can not receive tribute. All her religious hope is in the present arrangement. In India every household has its idol, and daily obeisence must be made as a protection from the evil eye and other misfortunes. Woman knows no god except through her husband, and the idea of a personality for herself is foreign to her. No pagan religion holds a high ideal for woman. Christianity demands that she have the right to stand before the altar with her brothers. It asks equality of individuality for her when her husband has been accustomed to think it a disgrace to speak of her otherwise than apologetically. Even Buddhism, the most humane of all pagan faiths, gives her a character of passivity and makes her a negative personality, the shadow of her husband. Her status is fixed religiously, and religion is the mightiest of conserving forces, as well as the greatest of dynamics in reform. Whether it will act as a dynamic or a static force depends upon its principles, and Christianity is the one great reformative faith.

Everywhere are the signs of awakening. Here again the missionary confers a vast benefit over and above the actual making of converts. The ideal of home and motherhood that he takes finds lodgement in the good soil of the better nature of men in heathenism and is bringing forth fruitage. Mere example is not enough. The Parsis have dwelt in Bombay for centuries, and their women have been given an equality with men and educated as their brothers have been. This fact, together with their rejection of caste, has made them superior among native Hindu peoples. But India passed them by without learning the lesson, and no Parsi would stoop to teach it, for his is not a missionary religion. But Christianity inculcates the lesson by entering into the hearts of men. It may not lift all conviction to the level of actual conversion to the church, but it lifts multitudes to the level of more humane custom and better ways of thinking. The Gaekwar of Baroda is not a Christian, but he is awake to the need of reforms in India, and is one of its most advanced rulers. He has broken caste by traveling abroad and openly preaches the superior social life of Christianity. As quoted by Robert Speer, in his "Christianity and the Nations," he says regarding India's women: "Early marriage must increase death and disease among mothers, swell infant mortality, and injure the physic of the race. A too strict Purdah mutilates social life and makes its current dull and sluggish by excluding the brightening influence of women. By denial of education to women we deprive ourselves of half the potential force of the nation, deny our children the advantage of having cultured mothers, and by stunting the faculties affect injuriously the heredity of the race." In Japan women are taking a place in intelligent society and in public affairs. In China a recent meeting to protest against the opium

92

Rahuni Vernacular School, Marathi Mission, West India. The boys are returning from their daily swim. All are taught English and a trade.

traffic was not only attended by women, but they participated in it on an equality with men. In India societies are now organized looking to the redemption of her position through raising the age for marriage, encouraging the marriage of widows, and providing for her education. The day of her emancipation is dawning, but Robert Speer says, "The non-Christian principles of class and sex inequality have ruled the whole world except where Christ has changed it."

4. THE DIVINE RIGHT OF CHILDHOOD.

In nothing does Christianity shine more resplendent by contrast than in its treatment of children and in its claims of natural right for them. When Jesus took the little ones in his arms and blessed them, he conferred upon childhood a benediction that has blessed it wherever his gospel has carried the good tidings of his emancipatory message. Heathenism is condemned by no one thing more than by its insensibility to human pain and the utter numbness of its sympathetic powers. In modern times, as in ancient, the rule of the pagan world is that the right of the father is supreme over the life of his offspring. The child is treated as the property of its parent, and its chance in life is bounded by his human interest in it. Under a culture that is so little characterized by the finer sentiments of humanity and that knows so little of charity, the rights of childhood can not be many. Sons have ever had the better chance in life, because of the selfish interests of the fathers. They have been privileged, not by any inherent rights of their own as human beings, but through the selfish concern of their fathers. Daughters have suffered the ignominy of being born females. In ancient times, as in modern, heathen parents valued them little if times were hard, or if luxury was great and their care a burden.

Quintillian said, "To kill a man is often held to be a crime, but to kill one's own children is sometimes considered a beautiful action among the Romans." In the midst of the city of Rome stood the Lactrian columns. At their feet children that were not wanted could be taken in the night, and to them came barterers in human flesh, to claim whatever their inhuman choice might prefer. Occasionally a childless woman might come to get consolation for her empty heart and take one of the exposed little ones to her motherly bosom; often men and women came to get for their households those whom they could make slaves or servants; more often the abandoned little ones fell into the maws of those inhuman beings who are willing to traffic in the flesh and blood of their kind and to rear children as they might cattle for lives of toil, or worse, that they might sell them into the shambles of shame. Those who placed them there knew what the results were to be, but they perhaps considered it better than the custom of strangling them to death with their own hands, or exposing them in the wilds for the beasts to prey upon. Most horrible of all it was not unknown for witches to seek their dead bodies that brains and vital parts might be used in their abominable incantations. Greece practiced what we have here noted of Rome. In neither country did a child have any standing before the law. Its life

94

was utterly in its father's hand. Under the Stoics some gain was made in obtaining natural rights, and the gradual enlightenment that time brought ameliorated their fate in custom, but little was really gained until Christianity struck the hearts of men with compassion and began to find lodgement in legal enactment, through the codes of Constantine and Justinian. The former ordered that when children could not be supported at home they should be brought to the officials and supported from the treasury. What such support was worth may be judged by the like provision made in modern China, where it is said the filth and squalor of government provided asylums are indescribable and the death rate high, while it is pitiful to hear the wails of the little orphans, half cared for at the hands of an officiary which knows no compassion beyond that imbibed from heathenism.

What was done by ancient heathenism is done by modern. There yet exists in China the towers into which parents could put their undesired little ones at night, and to which those who desired them for any purpose could come to obtain them. In famine times children are sold for a few shillings, and it is no uncommon sight to see the bodies of little girls exposed at the riverside. Infanticide is one of the most open and brazen of heathen customs. When in 1870 the registration of births was made compulsory in India, whole villages were found to have but one girl child to ten boys. In 1843 in one whole tribe not a female infant could be found. In whole provinces it was found that there was but one girl child to every six boys, and there are authorities who declare that to this day what can not be longer done in the open is done by stealth in innumerable cases. Poverty preys upon the bodies of children now as among the ancients, and poverty is one of the omnipresent phenomena of heathen lands. In the fourth century it reached the climax of its devastations in Rome, and all the laws of the empire were powerless to prevent the inherent paganism of the masses from practicing the olden horror. The same is true in modern India and China, and even more so among the untutored sons of barbarous lands.

, Among some tribes of Africa children born otherwise than according to prescribed custom are immediately killed. Some kill all twins, and most tribes make way with deformed or unnatural babes. The ancients destroyed their defective babes, or even worse, allowed them to be mangled that they might be used for begging, just as we are told is done in modern pagan lands where there is no Christian law to forbid. Seneca said: "Monstrous offspring we destroy. It is not anger but reason to thus separate the useless from the sound." Among the Gallas of Africa the custom is to throw any first-born child that happens to be a girl into the woods to die. Among other tribes all twins are destroyed. In the South Seas the missionaries found the strangling of infants one of the commonest of customs. In other places all born in certain seasons were destroyed, and there is scarce a barbarous land where is not found the practice of destroying child life with impunity. Heathenism is stricken with a lack of pity and dominated by the brutality of the strong. Gibbon says, "The exposi-

tion of children was the stubborn vice of antiquity."
It prevailed down until the fourth century in Rome,
and among the less tutored races of Europe until
Christianity gained authority over their consciences.
The sacrifice of children prevailed in Prussia until
within a thousand years of our own time. It prevails
until this day among peoples in a like stage of barbarism, wherever they may be on the earth. Christianity
is the only religion that champions the rights of the
little ones as their divine heritage. It is the only
religion that holds their example up as a type of the
better life and says, "A little child shall lead them."
It alone provides orphanages for them and punishes
crimes against their persons as against those of adults.
That which heathenism makes their offense, viz.,
their weakness, Christianity makes their defense, and
provides extra precaution for their protection.

But it is not in matters of life and death alone,
nor in the supreme authority of parents to barter and
sell them that they suffer in non-Christian lands. It
is a Chinese saying that there is a "pail of tears for
every bound foot." The suffering entailed upon millions of little almond-eyed girls by that cruel custom
can not be estimated. It was not sanctioned by Confucius, but is the social custom of centuries. To-day
Anti-Foot Binding Societies are thriving in China.
They were organized by missionary women and are
fostered by statesmen who acknowledge their debt
to the missionary. To have large feet in China is to
be out of fashion and to suffer that cruel ostracism
which Dame Fashion administers, even in Christian
lands, with terrible severity. Few desire such girls

in wedlock, and they are made a laughing stock and an object of jibes from their own sex. It will take time to uproot such a social custom, and no less a power than one that will, like Christianity, make it a matter of conscience can ever succeed. The pitiable case of the child widow in India was spoken of in a previous section of this chapter. Though the law now forbids the marriage of any child under the age of twelve, or before fourteen if protested, it is not enforced where native sentiment does not approve it.

The only relief for the child life of heathenism is the new valuation of life which Christianity brings. Even if the gross cruelties of sale and death are forbidden through a greater enlightenment, there will be no real emancipation until Christianity brings its divine right of childhood. In the midst of ancient society the church stood as the savior of child life. It forbade the exposure of little ones and made it a virtue to rescue them. It founded asylums and administered them for centuries before governments learned that the founding of such institutions were a part of their responsibility. In mission lands to-day the church does the same work. In famine times in India it has rescued its tens of thousands, and at all times has entered its note of protest against abhorrent custom. The supreme right of the father extended to maturity and beyond among the ancient pagans, just as it does to this day in modern China. He had the legal power of life and death and his will was supreme by the patriarchal law. It was not until Constantine wrote his code that the right to kill a son in punishment was denied, and not until in the days of

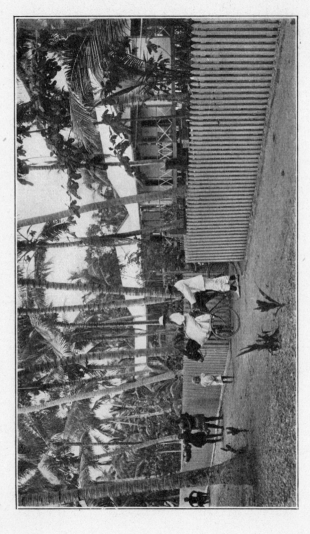

A Missionary Home in the Tropics. The architecture, sanitary surroundings, and garden cultivation are all models for the native community.

the more Christian laws of Justinian that a son was given rights to his own property. China is yet living in that ancient era so far as legal rights are concerned, but she is receiving a vast leaven from Christian influences and will recast more law and custom within the next generation than Rome did in three centuries. The church was small in Rome, but she brings with her the mighty impact of a Christianized civilization to these modern nations and the race will be more quickly run.

5. The Missionary Home a Social Center.

The missionary home is a sort of social settlement in the midst of the pagan community. The settlement idea is that of simply living and making a home in the midst of a neighborhood that has need of higher examples of living. The friendship of neighbors who will uplift and lend a helping hand is believed by settlement workers to be the primal means of effecting social good. They conceive of the home as being as much personal as institutional, and as the chiefest medium through which neighborly help can be extended. The settlement is a neighborhood house and to it all are welcome as friends, for through personal friendship religion reaches its most perfect social interpretation.

Some have said that the greatest single contribution of missions is that of the Christian home. If the home be the foundation-stone of order and progress in a civilization, and if non-Christian peoples are found to be most lacking in real home life, then the contribution of a model Christian home is, indeed, one of the chief contributions to be made to their social welfare and uplift. In it are found those exemplary characters which, however we may consider them as the most fundamental objects of Christian culture, are never made outside of association with other individuals, and whose virtues shine never so resplendently as in the intimacies of family life.

One missionary woman tells how she did her work through her home duties and preached without sermons through the medium of a quiet and home-like entertainment of her native neighbors. The door was ever open and the tea cup always ready. The housekeepers of the neighborhood were welcomed as friends, and sat them down for a friendly chat. Their familiar questions were her opportunities. They learned of the Christian ideals of home refinements and of sanitary housekeeping. She instructed them in the wifely arts of mending and fancy work and all manner of neat house wifery. Cooking came in for its share of talk, and many a lesson was given in hygienic preparation of foods. In these lessons, given through the natural interest of neighbors in her, to them, new and strange manner of living, she instructed them not to despise their own ways, but to add to them the universal needs of cleanliness, economy, harmony, beauty, neatness, and refinement. For it must be remembered that the missionary does not advocate the building of houses after the Western model, nor the changing of customs to agree with Western innovations, but only that the principles of better and more cleanly living be introduced into their ways, and that orderliness and sanitation be used in the practice of their native customs.

One of the curiosities of the missionary home to most of its neighbors is the honor and regard paid the wife by the husband, and the mutual life they live in their family relationships. Love is universally attractive. Peoples whose customs forbid any interchange of affection between husband and wife are attracted to the better way when they see it practiced by those whose probity they respect, and they come to comprehend that it is the way to a higher happiness. When husband and wife go abroad they walk side by side, while the pagan wife must ever keep to the rear, or go not at all when her husband goes; it excites comment and curiosity and not infrequently adverse criticism until it is better understood and more familiar to their eyes, but gradually it establishes a new regard for womankind, and in the course of time begins to break down the old and insidious practices of disrespect to which their wives have been accustomed from times immemorial. To lift one-half of humanity into the regard and social respect of the other half is a mighty achievement, and when that one-half is the motherhood of a race it is scarcely possible to measure its effects upon society.

The orderliness and refinement of the Christian home is usually in striking contrast to that of the lowly homes about it. In savage Africa houses are built low and small, without chimneys or windows, and the only means of entrance is through a low door that makes entering an acrobatic feat. Inside there is no furniture beyond a possible rude shelf or two, and a low bed of grass and mats. The floor is mud or the excreta of the herd, tramped hard with native feet, and the smoke of the fire fills the air as it seeks outlet through the thatched roof or open door. Inside there is anything but cleanliness, and the usual refinements of separating the sexes and providing for privacy, are unthought of. The patriarchal households of the more cultured peoples do not allow privacy, and the communal village life of the more barbarous tribes have never thought of it. In China and India the masses live, not in cities, nor in isolated farm-houses, as do Americans, nor yet in separate yards, as we do in our town life, but in small villages. Their streets are narrow alleyways or an unkept country road, and the small and unkempt houses are builded close against each other. The roofs are low, the street line irregular, the open spaces uncared for and full of filth. There is no regularity of outline in things, and everything bears the impress of disorder. Privacy is not maintained in separated family living. Every one knows every one else's business, and the chief diversion of the settlement is gossip. There is but one well, and to it both humans and animals repair indiscriminately. In India it may be a great tank or pool, and cattle and men alike frequent it for the quenching of thirst; all repair there for the provision of cooking water, the doing of the village washing, and to find a common center for the village life. The unspeakable sanitary conditions can be better imagined than described, and the appalling death rate that obtains among children needs little further explanation.

THE HOME

In striking contrast, the village of the native Christian community stands as an illustration of how Christianity redeems the home life. It is not a paradise of beauty and refinement, but it is a vast improvement over the old manner of family life. The dwelling-places are cleaner and the children clothed with regard for modesty; the walls are upright and the roofs in better repair; the floors may still be of earth, but they are more cleanly, and modern conveniences are introduced with due regard to the meagerness of the native income; there is a more industrious type of life, especially among the barbarous peoples, for one of the things that Christianity takes to them is incentive to work, and a desire for more of the utensils of civilization. The heathen home is merely a place to get shelter. In tropical lands much of the cooking and most of the living is done out of doors, and in that is the best protection they have from their dwelling-places; otherwise all would surely be afflicted with disease, and death would be epidemic. In agricultural lands the animals usually live under the same roof with their owners; man and beast can not thus dwell together with aught but injury for the man. The native Christians may work at the same tasks, follow the same general customs, receive the same wage, and practice the same economic arts that they did in their old life, but they live more wholesomely in the midst of the old tasks and surroundings. Their children are clothed and their homes places of peace; their wages are kept for family purposes and never wasted on personal vices; their homes take on an angle of uprightness both within and without; the streets are cleaner and a more sanitary manner of life is followed; their wives are treated with kindness, and affection begins to root in their hearts where all too often there was none before; they love peace where before discord was the habit of their daily family intercourse; in fact, their home has taken the likeness of the missionary home, their village bears witness externally to the internal changes in their minds and hearts, and travelers say it is easy to tell the village where Christian influence predominates. It is a living testimony to the social value of missions. "It is refreshing to see the clean houses and villages of the Christians, instead of the filthy heathen hovels of previous years," said Dr. McKay.

In the mission home the family find their chief delight in the congenial converse of the table around the family hearthstone. The pagan family knows little of family counsel or mutual conversation about a family shrine, such as the missioner makes his board and hearth. Rarely does a Chinese child ever dine with both father and mother. The father is privileged over other members of the household, and the male members of the circle are accustomed to eating in the congenial company of their superior selves. The language of the heathen household is anything but pure and refined. Children learn talk that put the blush to men's faces, and the customary quarreling is carried from the house into the street. The father holds the scepter over both mother and children, and the mother-in-law over the wives of her sons. Arbitrariness is much more the rule than kindness, and the result is a bitterness in word and feeling and in mutual action that is liable to result in blows. Until this day instances are not unknown where parents have beaten children into insensibility and even sold them deliberately to be rid of them, or to purchase opium. The Christian home reproves this sort of a family life, and the benign example of Christian affection and peacefulness arouse in many hearts a longing for the better way. The men of the community come to respect the wife of the missionary because of her talents, for the interest she takes in their homes, and because they see her respected by her husband. Through the open channels of this regard for her, and through the undeniable argument of a greater happiness through it, many who before treated their women with scant regard or only conventional affection, come to open their hearts and overcome their ancient customs and accord her a real love, and to surround their children with a more refined and wholesome moral atmosphere. The tendency is well fixed, both in China and India, for the family to divide into its logical units and each married couple to have a separate dwelling-place and a division of income. Greater privacy is being guaranteed, and with it must come the more dignified manner of living and the cultivating of those personal virtues that arise from a greater sense of individuality and of personal rights.

Thus from the missionary's home radiate sermons from actions and an atmosphere that is conducive to social health. Its example is eloquent to the very human consciousness of its neighbors, and its exhortations, though mutely spoken, are more persuasive oftentime than an articulate message. To become a neighbor to a man is to fulfill the law of service toward him. In the Christian home are the head waters of all that fructifies the rich fields of civilization, and no greater judgment of failure could be pronounced upon a society than to say, as has been said of heathenism, that it has no homes. Ten thousand missionary homes are bearing their witness on the mission field, and the social benefits that flow from that witness are mightier than words can tell; there is no statistic that is able to enumerate the unbounded good they are bringing to the new civilizations that spring up wherever they are founded.

CHAPTER III

Benevolence: The Heart of Social Progress

1. THE EVANGEL OF HUMANITY.

Benevolence is the heart of social progress. It is through the expanding circles of sympathy that civilization evolves. The primitive man is selfish; it is his kinship to the brute. Sympathy is all but unknown to him except as it reacts very directly upon his own welfare. But mother love softens the heart of the rudest, and its expansion into family affection widens the circle of sympathy and broadens unselfishness; it is nature's first instinct of sacrifice. Mother love expands into brother love. The interwoven interests of family merge into those of tribe, clan, neighborhood, and nation, and finally become universal. Every stage of civilization manifests some measure of this larger bond of common interest. China is to-day no farther advanced than was the world to which the first missionaries went. Africa is but at the dawn of human evolution, if indeed it be not a decadent continent of people. Paton, Hunt, Geddie, Williams, and their compeers found humanity in the South Pacific Seas almost devoid of the instinct of sympathy. Japan had evolved a paternalistic type of society, and cared for the suffering with more effectiveness than any other pagan nation. In the change from the old to the new, the old system was overthrown and the new is being established, substituting national for the feudal care of the dependent. The Chinese, says Arthur Smith, "display an indifference to the suffering of others which is probably not to be matched in any other civilized country." They have never evolved more than a family type of sympathy, except where they have come into contact with Christianity. Their naturally fine capacity as a people quickly yields to those higher compassions that are native to their nature but have never been cultivated. In India the caste to which one belongs is alone responsible for him. There are fifty millions of low caste and out-caste peoples who have no one to care for them. Paganism has no deep sympathies and the circles of human responsibility are small. Neither their governments nor their religions furnish such a thing as real philanthropy. Old Rome fed thousands at the public granaries, but there was no organized charity; it was more an act of political expediency than of public benevolence. In many Oriental cities, including the Mohammedan, there are small institutions supported by subscription from the rich, but they are few in number and so poorly managed that they count for little. Even in Japan the amount of public relief is less than one hundredth as much per capita as it is in America, and the need is many times as great. The mark of progress in civilization is the breadth of its interests. The "struggle for self" gives over increasingly to the "struggle for others." Pagan Rome grew great by the growth of imperialism and by the creation of a few great through their power over the exploited many; but its luxury and heartlessness were its ruin. In the fourth century poverty was perhaps the greatest it has ever been in Western civilization. In the midst of it all Christianity grew up with marvelous rapidity through its benevolence and its appeal to the common man. Rome apotheosized wealth and power; Christianity worshiped a Carpenter who had "not where to lay his head." Rome's divinity was a luxurious and dissipated Caesar; Christianity's was a pure and humble Nazarene. Rome subdued a world by force of arms; Christianity by the force of brotherly love.

The non-Christian world is poverty-stricken. The Hon. Chester Holcomb said that if modern American almshouses were to be erected in China and thrown open to all who would come, two-thirds of the population would be at their doors, because what they would receive there would be so much better than what they live on all their lives. Bishop Thoburn says that one-fourth of the Hindu people live without enough to nourish their bodies properly, and that millions are always on the borderland of starvation. The wages of the common laborer in all these countries will average less than one-tenth that of the same toiler in our own land. In India men work for from six to twelve cents per day, and women at from three to four. In Japan wages are not more than twice as much, and in China they are no better; servants will work for three or four dollars per month and support themselves. The average for school teachers is but from fifty to sixty dollars per annum. It is not enough to say that living is cheap. It is not cheap living, but a low standard of living that makes life at all possible to ninety per cent of the people of the pagan world. In three thousand years of civilization, Japan, India, and China evolved no standard of living that gave them title to human prosperity, and the standard of living is the mark of economic progress; upon it hangs the possibility of all other progress; it is the base line of civilization.

Where there is so little margin for a livelihood there is great suffering when famine comes. In the seventies no less than ten million died in the Chinese famine. India made little progress in population until England stopped the awful devastations of death that came with her drouths, by building irrigating ditches and providing public relief works and teaching the farmers how to conserve their lands; in one famine she spent no less than thirty million dollars in relief. Neither India nor China ever made any preparation to meet nor any adequate effort to relieve these awful holocausts of death. "There are millions more," said a Chinese official when his sympathy was asked for these famine sufferers; he was an untutored Malthusian. In India one province suffers while another has plenty, but there is no connection established between the granaries of the prosperous district and the lazar house of the famine ridden, except as Christian charity brings the price.

Buddhist priests are to-day making some agitation for charity in the name of Gautama. Like Julian, the apostate emperor, they rally their coreligionists with the cry, "It is a scandal that the Galileans should

110

*H*ospital at Hanyang, China. It illustrates the commodiousness and modern type of the best class of missionary institutions.

support the destitute, not only of their own religion, but of ours." The Brahmans care for the sacred cow, but they do not erect homes for orphans or asylums for lepers. Christianity cares for a million each year in the very midst of these pagan faiths. In India alone it has eight thousand orphan and famine children in its homes and industrial schools. Where the pagan religions do any charity it is for the purpose of obtaining merit. Brahmanism denies the privilege of erecting institutions because the merit is in the secrecy of the gift; thus a very small coin to the beggar or a bowl of rice to the fakir suffices. Lecky says Christianity's power as a civilizing factor has been in its "capacity for producing a disinterested enthusiasm." He says the Christian religion has "done more to quicken the affections of mankind, to promote pity, to create a pure and merciful ideal, than any other influence that ever acted upon the world." It has ever appealed to the poor and needy and dispossessed of the earth, and from them has created the rulers of the next age. Its famine children go from their schools to create a new type of home and industry, and to lead with a new and benign intelligence in the common affairs of their fellows. It lights the fires of sympathy in humble hearts and the contagion spreads from their humble habitations into the hearts and homes of their neighbors, and the old customs of cruelty, callousness, and superstition are displaced in society. In the South Seas men who once would have robbed and eaten the shipwrecked, have been known to rescue and succor them. In Dark Africa tribes that were ever at war have carried relief to one another in time of distress. In the far North peoples who once killed their aged have come to care for them tenderly. Wherever the missionary goes he lights the beacon fires for the distressed and suffering, and offers them hope in the name of the Christ who healed the sick, cleansed the lepers, blessed the children, befriended womankind, and preached good tidings to the poor.

There are some practices of heathenism that are almost too cruel and revolting to seem possible. Cannibalism is yet practiced in parts of Africa, in New Guinea, and in several islands of Micronesia. The aborigines of Australia were found indulging the horrible practice as late as 1896. In many places pioneer missioners have lived to see cannibal chieftains die Christian. One young worldling visited in the South Seas, carrying with him a blasé sneer for the missionary. He was shown a hollow tree, enclosing a heap of several hundred stones, and told by his native guide that each one represented a human body that had been served before the late chieftain, and that but for the missionary one would represent him there on the morrow. Paton, Geddie, Hunt, Chalmers, and many others wrought new creations among cannibal peoples and transformed places of such unspeakable savagery into islands of peace. The Fijians contributed liberally to one of the late Indian famines, and are to-day the best church goers in the world, unless it be, perhaps, the slave-hunting tribes of Uganda, whom Mackay and his successors converted into disciples of brotherly love. Holcombe tells of the horrible manner in which the people of Peking disposed of their dead babies. They cared for them until hope grew faint. They then placed them upon the door step and awaited the issue; if they died they were accounted no children of theirs; in the early mornings a great wagon made the rounds, gathering up the little bodies, and they were sent away without funeral or tear. In parts of Africa the lepers are killed. The Esquimaux of Alaska were found making a holiday out of the killing of their aged. The beggars of Chinese cities are carted out for the dogs to eat, or left where they die. Many Hindus carry their dying out of the house as soon as death seems imminent, and if possible, carry them to the banks of the sacred Ganges to gasp out their expiring moments. It is a common custom to begin funeral preparations before life is gone. Paganism lacks the finer sentiments even where it does not possess the most gross. Its circle of sympathy is small. Christianity takes to it the message of universal brotherhood and gives it a heart for humanity.

2. CLINICAL CHRISTIANITY.

"All missionary work, in the highest sense, must be healing work," said the indomitable Mackay of Uganda. Mackay used medicine, industrial training, carpentry, diplomatic advice, and all other means that opportunity offered to break his way into the confidences of M'tesa and overcome the frightful cruelties of that cruel chieftain's slave traffic, and the even more frightful superstitions that made all other evils possible. After a lifetime in Africa the great Frenchman, Coillard, wished he had another life that he might study medicine and spend it in the

8 113

Dark Continent, opening fastened doors, and, like Livingstone before him, probe roads of healing into the open sores of Africa's savagery.

The new physiology makes the body sacred, even as Christ did when he declared it to be the temple of the Spirit. The new psychology knits mind and body up together in such manner as to make consideration of one impossible without a knowledge of the other. The new ethics demands the sacredness of the flesh as a means to the holiness of the soul, and our understanding of Christianity, in these latter days, leads us to see that there is not only no antagonism between spirit and body, but that there is a divine relationship. Asceticism revolted against the frightful immoralities of base paganism and swung to the extreme of despising the body, but we find that not emaciation but emancipation is the true way of life. Thus we seek, religiously, to free ourselves of disease and to live a clean and wholesome life, and we find in good hygiene one of the ways to upright living.

Jesus healed as he preached. Indeed, there is as much emphasis given in the synoptic gospels to his healing as to his preaching. The deaf, blind, dumb, lame, fevered, epileptic, insane, all received his merciful ministrations. He sought out the suffering and the suffering sought out him. Multitudes brought of their sick that he might touch them and make them well. His great-hearted sympathy went out in compassion in the divine ministry of destroying pain. It was his care for the suffering of bodily ills that made him known above all as the man of compassion. That greatest of all encomiums pronounced upon him, de-

114

scribing him as one who went about doing good, was due to his ministry to pain. One of his most used, because most significant titles, that of the Great Physician, comes from his cure of physical ills. He never conceived of his gospel being preached without ministration to the physical needs of the poor and suffering. When he sent out his disciples for their itineraries, he told them to go healing and preaching.

The masses of men live very much in their physical beings. Not many are able to arise above pain and become saints and poets in spite of it. It is difficult to be both a sufferer and a saint, or to be poor and practice the refinements of Christianity. That it is possible is unanswerable testimony to the spiritual power of a true faith, but Christ did not intend that poverty and suffering were to be made cardinal means to righteousness. He intended rather that through the relief of them Christianity should take the world. The great world of paganism is a world of ignorance and of spiritual numbness. It lives in the flesh, and finds its first revelations most easily by relief of its pains. "If we want," says Dr. Arthur Lankaster, "to write the teaching of our Lord Jesus Christ in very large letters, so that those who can not read theology and do not understand science or philosophy can read it very easily, the best way of doing it, whether it be for an individual, a village, a town, a district, or a nation, is to start medical aid for the poor." "He is not from America, he is from heaven," said the astonished Korean courtiers when Dr. Allen stopped the wounds of their dying crown prince. It was a sermon without words, but a thousand times more eloquent to their ears than could any have been in words. To-day all Korea is listening to the words of the evangelists. He may throw our proffered Bible aside, said Dr. Williamson, our civilization make him all the more a materialist, and we may be unable to convince him that we are not preaching for the sake of the salary, but heal his disease and ease his suffering and he is eternally grateful, and through his friendship for you will learn of that greater friend. Science can be cold and heartless in its quest of mere knowledge, but science, set on fire with compassion for men, is one of God's means of revealing himself to those who are dumb to all other appeals.

Medicine takes a new humanitarianism to the peoples who have not known the sacred art of sympathy. The Hindu religion will lead its devotees to swing themselves by hooks in the back, or sit for days on beds of spikes, or to spend $50,000 on the wedding of a pair of sacred monkeys, but it never built a hospital. "In all my classical reading," said Professor Packard, "I never met with the idea of an infirmary or hospital, except for sick cats in Egypt." Certain sects of Hindu devotees will not sit down without first brushing the earth lest they destroy some insect life, villages will see their children die by serpent and tiger and refuse to kill the beast because its life is sacred, but women suffer untold miseries when children are born, little ones starve by the tens of thousands in famine times, beggars perish and rot by the wayside, for their faith has taught them no such ideas of the value of a human life as to lead them to organize charities, or build asylums, or create systematic forms of

116

relief. Multitudes suffer from preventable disease, but there is no adequate art devised for their healing, and even such physicians as they have will refuse them aid because they are too poor to pay. Medicine, in the hands of a missionary, opens to them new visions of the sacredness of life itself. The native Christians will care for the poorest and the foulest of their fellow-men, where before they would have passed them by with no thought, or mayhap joined the crowd in jibes at their sad predicament. It was no different among the ancient pagans. "Among the millionaires of Rome there was not one who founded a hospice for the poor or a hospital for the sick," said Dr. Dollinger. They had culture and philosophy and art, but they had no adequate humanity. Their lives were ordered from the standpoint of selfishness. The most learned, and those who speculated profoundly about the soul and its future, could, with no pang, consign the multitudes to a place beside animals and argue that they were born to be slaves—men who, by their very nature, could never realize on a human inheritance.

Of modern religions the most compassionate is Buddhism. There is record of a Buddhist hospital three hundred years before Christ, but that religion is so profoundly individualistic that it soon lost all power for real charity. Its main sanction was that of merit for self, and until men forgot self and self's reward they are never of great value to benevolence. From the first Christianity practiced a self-forgetful charity, and began to build institutions for the public care of the sick by the end of the first thousand years of its

117

history. Before that they had received care in monasteries and at private hands, and the law had taken account of them from the time it began to take account of Christian principles. It is under Christian governments that philanthropic institutions are builded today, and those of Japan and the few instances in China are due to Christianity's having come to teach the way.

Dr. Gulick quotes a noted Japanese of the era of the first Catholic missions in that land as saying that "people contribute to the temple, but never before was it heard that a temple contributed to the help of the people." Medicine takes a new conception of religion in its enforcement of the missionary, and reduces the precept to example in a manner that can not be misunderstood by the most ignorant and prejudiced of superstitious minds. "Missionary medicine has not exhausted its influence when it has healed the sick one," says Dr. Williamson in his excellent little volume on "The Healing of the Nations;" "it reaches round and exerts its power on a larger world than that gathered in the hospital waiting room. It pioneers education; it stimulates scientific methods; it inculcates sanitary principles and introduces plague precautions and deals with epidemics. Again and again it becomes of political importance; its weight is thrown on the side of benevolent undertakings, while all the time it is raising in estimation the value of human life and the sacredness of womanhood. These are stars of the first magnitude which shine brightly in the firmament of Christian Sociology." The itinerary of the medical missionary resembles the evangelistic journeys of the

118

*K*oords, Syrians, and Moslems in a Missionary Clinic. Illustrates the manner in which Christian benevolence breaks
down prejudice.

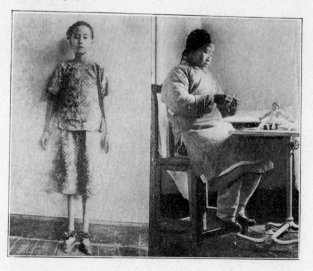

A Chinese orphan girl before and after treatment in a missionary hospital. This is a parable of Christian benevolence on the mission field.

Great Physician. Men come miles to meet him and his roadway is the scene of many pitiful appeals; he touches one here and another there and leaves his healing balm in a hundred hands every day; he healeth their diseases and to every one gives the greater prescription for the cure of the soul. His dispensary and hospital waiting-room are like the evenings at the lakeside in Galilee, where the multitudes brought their sick and afflicted that the Great Physician might touch them. There come the rich and poor to mingle side by side, for a great need doth make brothers of them all, and all receive, that through the healing of their bodies their souls may be freed.

3. THE DEVASTATIONS OF IGNORANCE.

There is no science of medicine in the non-Christian world. In savage lands, and often in the Orient, the profession is mingled with the black arts and the profession of witchery. In Africa it is in the hands of women who deal in charlatanry, or of the medicine man, who is adept in magic and generally the greatest fraud and scoundrel in the tribe. He "smells" out the trouble with all due ceremony and locates it in the ill will of some enemy or the displeasure of some spirit. His cure is one of propitiation for the offended spirit, or of "ordeal" for the enemy who has done bewitching. "Evil eye" is the fertile cause of many of the diseases of superstition. It hedges life around with unending regulation, and makes living a terror. It indicts many an innocent person with the crime of bewitching and is the source of untold enmity and of punishment that is undeserved. In China the physicians have many simple herbal remedies that observation has taught them to be useful, but they are so mixed with the rites of superstition, or the prescriptions of a credulous ignorance, that they are largely deprived of their virtue in actual practice. All ignorance is dangerous, but nowhere does it bring more direct suffering than in the practice of medicine. A lady physician in Persia tells of seeing a native quack burn open the frontal fissure in the head of an infant that the evil spirit might escape. Another in Korea tells of seeing a native practitioner burn heaps of brown powder on the breast of a child and follow it by thrusting a large needle through each foot, the palms of the hands, the thumb joints, the lips, and then beneath the nose. A doctor in India tells of a mother who brought a child to him for treatment of the eyes, saying she had faithfully followed the prescription every day for two months; it was to put a powder of charcoal and donkey's tooth into the eye. For suppuration it is customary to daub tar or some other adhesive over the place where the puss should exude; the agony that follows can well be imagined. One Chinese cure for hysteria is to put bugs up the nose of the victim. Rheumatism is often treated by cutting a gash over the aching joint and rubbing cayenne pepper into the wound, which is then bound up. The native Chinese quack will thrust a long, rusty needle into the affected part, to allow the evil spirit to escape and then burn the wound to heal it. The liver is looked upon as the source of many ills and the people are much given to stomach trouble; both organs as

well as the lungs receive the wicked needle when affected. Gongs are beaten to drive away the demons,
and the most hideous noises are raised where good
treatment demands quiet. Many crowd around and
touch with their filthy hands and clothes, when isolation is demanded by aseptic necessity. Dr. Keeler,
of Changli, tells of one man who came to him with
four hundred punctures of the Chinese needle in the
spine and thighs. Hindu mothers will be confined to a
dirty hut for days after the birth of their children and
compelled to go without either food or water, and then
be given a cold bath. One Chinaman had tried to cure
dyspepsia by a two years' course of drinking daily
a cup of ground stone and water; he had taken forty
pounds off a grindstone, but was uncured. It is not
simply the suffering that is uncured, but that which
is caused in the use of ignorance and superstition, that
cries out for a scientific medical profession in pagan
lands.

The native practitioner has no education for his
work and is quite as liable to be the most ignorant and
unsuccessful man of the community as any other.
There is no knowledge of anatomy and little of materia
medica. Dissection is unheard of and would be looked
upon with horror in the Orient. The Chinese believe
there are five tubes leading from the mouth to the
stomach, and that both lungs are on one side. The
Hindus say there are nine hundred bones in the human
body. There is no adequate diagnosis; it is largely a
matter of guess work or of an attempt to locate the
demon. Their prescriptions are fearfully and wonder-

fully made. Here is a sample as reported by a missionary physician:

Powdered snake.....................	2 parts
Wasps and their nests...............	1 part
Centipedes........................	6 parts
Scorpions..........................	4 parts
Toads.............................	20 parts

Grind thoroughly, mix with honey, and
    make into pills.
Dose, two to be taken four times a day.

Tiger's bones are a sovereign remedy for weakness and for cowardice, because the tiger is strong and brave. Bugs, beetles, flies, bats, and lizards are common remedies. In extreme cases in China the flesh of a son or daughter has been prescribed; it would be good for the child as well as the parent, for it would thereby learn filial obedience. In savage lands charms are used, drums beaten, horns blown, and various devices resorted to for the overcoming of the demon. Some of the blood of the patient may be extracted and given to an animal that he may carry the spirit away and get the benefit of its residence. It may be hoodooed into the anatomy of some special enemy, or it may be extracted by the legerdemain of the medicine man and held up to the view of wondering relatives in the form of a bug or snake or some small varmint which he has deftly extracted from his sleeve.

The death-rate of children is appalling in lands that have no scientific medicament. The rate for little ones of one year and under is twice as great in Calcutta as it is in London; Calcutta is one of the most

modern of Oriental cities and London one of the most
congested of those in the Occident. The normal
death-rate for non-Christian lands is twice that of
Christian countries. It would be much worse but for
the habit semi-barbarous peoples have of living
out of doors. In Asia the masses drink hot tea to
the exclusion of water to such an extent that they
are saved from the ravages of the germ-laden streams
and ponds to which the majority repair for use of
kitchen and washtub.

Smallpox has decimated islands in the South Seas
and taken one-half the populations in Oriental communities; it was thought to be the devastation of
demons; one-half the deaths in Korea are through it.
The United States has banished it from its realm, so
far as epidemics are concerned, by the use of vaccination, and our physicians fear measles more than they
do the once dreaded scourge of smallpox; but it destroys with all its terrors where cleanliness is not a
virtue and there is no knowledge of the nature of disease and its transmitting qualities. In the city of
Canton the population seems to be a pox-marked
people, as if it were a racial peculiarity. One meets
the disease in all its forms on the street in mid-day.
The even more terrible scourges of cholera and the
bubonic plague have worked their way unhindered
until in very recent years, and the measures taken
now are the result of the work of the medical missionary, except perhaps in the case of India. "How is it
that you Christians do not take the plague?" said an
intelligent Chinaman, "we have had processions and
fire-crackers, and made presents to our gods, but all

in vain; we are dying by the hundreds." A village in India recently filled the trees about its environs with the bodies of decapitated dogs, that the spirits might be frightened away as they came to bring the plague. In Tibet the heroic expedient of burning the poor first victims of smallpox is sometimes resorted to. Cholera is one of the most easily avoided of epidemics. It can be conveyed only through a very specific contamination, and one that endangers no one where every one is cleanly. Dr. Osgood says that 60% of the diseases the medical missionary meets are those due to uncleanliness. There is no knowledge of sanitation nor of disease germs. An Oriental city smells with the seventy-odd smells Coleridge found in old Cologne. The nasal organs of the East are benumbed. Sewage is dumped in the street and left for dogs to eat. Stagnant water stands before houses and in village streets. Drainage is unknown except where civilization has first gone. Light is not one of the household commodities and fresh air is not prized for its own sake. A medical missionary in Persia says that his patients fear both open windows and light. Mecca is a menace to all India and Eastern Asia; contagion spreads from almost every pilgrimage. The pilgrims are filthy and huddle in crowded quarters while in the sacred city. Whatever happens is by the will of Allah, and precautions are scorned. The *Lancet* gives an incident that illustrates the attitude of a Moslem mind toward hygienic regulations. The French Government desired to obtain certain information about Moslem cities for the use of its colonial office. The following questions were sent to the ruling Pasha of Damascus, and the answers here given were returned:

"What is the death-rate per thousand in your principal city?"

Ans. "In Damascus it is the will of Allah that all should die; some die old, some die young."

"Are the supplies of drinking water sufficient and of good quality?"

Ans. "From the remotest period no one has died of thirst."

"Make general remarks on the hygienic condition of your city."

Ans. "Since Allah sent us Mohammed, his prophet, to purge the world with fire and sword, there has been a vast improvement. And now, my lamb of the West, cease your questioning. Man should not bother himself about matters that concern only God."

Perhaps no tragedy of ignorance is greater than that of the lepers and the insane among non-scientific peoples. As in Biblical times, the insane are looked upon as possessed with demons and are turned out to wander; they are shunned as were the lepers who had to cry, "unclean, unclean," at the approach of any one. Cases are known of them being walled up until death brought release. Violent cases are bound down and left with an occasional morsel. Refractory ones are beaten, and the custom generally is to accord them brutal treatment. On the other hand, some peoples look upon them as inspired. Demon worshipers stand in awe of them, and their sayings are regarded as divinations. In all the non-Christian world there is no record of a single infirmary for their protection or cure, except as the missionary gives it. Lepers meet a universal fate of isolation, with no hope, especially after the disease is marked or known by others. It may be hidden by the poor victim until he has inocculated many others, for leprosy, like many other transmittable diseases, is infectious rather than contagious.

Blindness is one of the most universal ills of pagan lands. There are a million blind in India and China alone. Little babes are bound to the back or over the hip of the mother or a little sister, and carried about with their tender eyes exposed to the tropical sun. Uncleanness is the prolific source of blindness as of all other diseases. The habit of having the barber cleanse the eyes is, in China, the source of much trouble, for he wipes the tender organ with his dirty and contaminated apron. Again, lack of precaution spreads the maladies. Necrosis of the feet, through footbinding, causes untold agonies among China's girls. Suffering of all kinds drives multitudes to the relief that opium can give. The deadly pipe habit is growing rapidly in India. There are numerous other specific ills that space does not allow named, but whose presence, and the devastation they wreak, can be laid up to habits of uncleanness and to ignorance of the nature of disease. Paganism has many diseases, but no adequate remedies for them. It has a penury as great as its other suffering, but it has neither hospital, scientific medicine, nor a charity that seeks the things of others as one's own.

126

4. ONE MULTIPLIED BY A THOUSAND.

In China there is but one scientific physician to every million souls. In the United States there is one to every six hundred. If there were but two doctors in Chicago, and one in St. Louis, we would have some idea of the needs of China and of the stupendousness of the medical missioner's work. In all paganism there is only one trained physician to every two and one-half million people. The average number of people within the radius of a mission station is probably twenty-five thousand. There are eight hundred medical missionaries. Thus they are able to reach in some adequate way about twenty million people. Their work spreads far beyond their stations, however. Patients have come journeys of weeks to receive healing. When Dr. Dye went to the Congo there was not another physician in a radius of eight hundred miles of Bolenge. Men came four hundred miles to his clinic. It is no uncommon thing for them to come from one hundred to one hundred and fifty miles. In China many instances are cited of them wheeling a member of the family a week's journey in the native barrow that they might get the benefit of a surgical operation. Three million patients are treated annually in the eleven hundred hospitals and dispensaries. A day's treatments will often include from one hundred to two hundred patients. One blind man who was cured went home and sent twelve blind neighbors to the physician. They came as of old, one leading the other. Another put twenty into a boat and had them taken to his benefactor. Every man helped

127

becomes an emissary of healing. The benevolence of the mission station reaches out for vast distances, and everywhere it goes it strikes a blow at the superstition of demon worship and the black ignorance of the natives.

The work done by some single medical missionaries and at certain hospitals all but defies credulity. The greatest practitioners and the most adequately equipped of the great hospitals at home do not equal it. In fifteen years Dr. Elizabeth Reifsnyder, of Shanghai, ministered to more than 200,000 patients. Dr. Butchart, of Lu Cheo Fu, is at present administering 35,000 treatments annually. Dr. John Kerr, of Canton, attended over 700,000 individuals in his work as a good physician in China, and performed 40,000 operations. The two hospitals in Canton give 112,000 treatments annually. In Swatow one missionary hospital receives into its beds 25,000 sick each year. The two Canton institutions have ministered to more than 1,250,000 persons since their establishment. But figures do not tell the story; they must be touched with imagination to convey any adequate picture of the work really done. One must see the long journeys by foot, boat, barrow, and mule-back to get to the missionary station, and think of the suffering endured under these primitive means of locomotion. He must picture the long and painful treatment endured often at the hands of the native quack before enough light reaches the poor sufferer to permit his prejudice, or that of his relatives, to send him to the foreigner. He must paint the scene in the waiting-room, the ulcerated limbs, the great tumors, the swollen bodies, the blind eyes, the wan and ghastly yellow faces, the torture of little children, the patient suffering of aged women whose whole life has been one of such hardship that pain no longer puzzles them. There the rich sit in their silks by the side of the beggar in his rags, and all look with the one human hope to the door into which they will soon enter, half in fear, half in awe, for the doctor seems to many of them to be a miracle worker.

But the medical man's work is not told even in the stupendous work he does with the multitudes that seek him, once he has won his way through the maze and mire of superstition. He goes into the broader field of social welfare and grapples with questions of sanitation, hygiene, and the establishment of governmental institutions for doing the work he is able only to begin doing. Dr. Berry taught a class of one hundred and twenty young men while doing the work of a strenuous medical missionary in Japan. Dr. Hepburn was the founder of medical science in Japan, and added to his missionary labors, not only instruction for a future profession in the empire, but every form of philanthropic effort, and was decorated by the Mikado for his gifts to the social welfare of the nascent nation. Dr. Mackenzie founded the first medical school in China, at Tientsin. The mother of Li Hung Chang gave him the first thousand dollars ever given by a native for Christian effort. The famous viceroy himself aided in all Mackenzie's work. The college is to-day under native auspices and the pioneer missionary's pupils are on its staff. The first lesson of the native doctor is to learn the location of the two

9   129

hundred places where punctures may be made with his long needle, without killing. In the modern missionary medical school he learns to perform surgical operations with skill. Japanese surgeons are among the famous operators of the world to-day, and China's will be in another generation. Dr. Tenny tells of thirty-two medical schools under missionary auspices. As in Japan, so it will soon be in China, the missionary will have established the idea of a scientific medical profession, and the nation will adequately endow its own schools for the training of a native profession in modern medicine and surgery.

The medical missionary writes pamphlets and books for public instruction and scatters them broadcast. His field is wide for this kind of work, for the ills of the land are more than one-half preventable by ordinary cleanliness and hygienic living. He studies climatic and other diseases peculiar to his chosen field, and thus adds to the sum total of medical knowledge. He learns the pharmacopœia of his district, that the people may have the benefit of cheaper medicines and the world the benefit of any discoveries that may be made. He prepares the public mind for dealing with epidemics and plagues, by lecturing and writing on ways to prevent them and means for dealing with them when they come. Governments listen to this instruction on such matters, and his power is multiplied by thousands. He establishes plague-camps and isolates all who will submit, that they may not be a menace to others, and may get the cure that pure air, water, and food will bring, together with his treatments. In Kashmir one physician sent the school boys out with tracts when the plague threatened, and they were purchased and heeded by hundreds. He introduces vaccination and has persuaded the government of Siam, through its enlightened late ruler, Chulalongkorn, to make it compulsory; to-day every child in Siam and Laos is vaccinated just as he is in America. One missionary station cared for more than 10,000, and Drs. Adamson and Braddock, of the Baptist Mission, superintended the vaccination of 200,000 in one year. He introduces modern surgical instruments, and many of the better native doctors learn both to use them for simple operations and to adopt his simpler remedies in their practice. Antiseptics, anesthetics, clinical thermometers, the art of nursing, and instruments for a more scientific diagnosis are all contributed by him to the better care and cure of the multitudes who are tortured with many irritating little ills due to their unhygienic living, and by many major evils that grow out of neglect or malpractice. In the late plague in China he induced the authorities to establish quarantines, and made inocculations that helped to get control of the situation. He convinces authorities of the benefits of the disinfectant and the necessity of the sewer, and in every way multiplies his force by enlisting newly enlightened public sentiment. Such work is a task of a lifetime, but once done, it is done forever.

The medical missionary is no longer needed in Japan, except as he is needed in our city slums and among the poor. In another generation or two this will be true of China and every land that has begun in earnest the work of public education. It was a millennium before the church received the help of governments in the tasks of social welfare, such as equipping hospitals, the care of the poor, the building of asylums, and the instruction of the youth. She must yet do much of it, but the more rapidly society takes over the task, the better is the work of the church done in bringing in the Kingdom of God. The governments in mission fields have the example of those of Christendom and will move more rapidly. Japan is in the lead, but there is no adequate institutional equipment there yet. China is beginning such work, and her statesmen acknowledge the debt of the nation to the missionary for showing them the way. Dr. John Kerr established the first infirmary for the insane in all China within the last decade. Dr. Berry is the father of prison reform in Japan; it is woefully inadequate yet, but the work of native Christians, like Haro, Ito, Tomeoka, and Oinue, has done much. Dr. Murray established the first school for the blind in China; his work is duplicated by several other missions to-day, but there is little by any but the Christians. In India, with its two hundred years of white rule, only one in twenty is yet reached by scientific medicine. Something more is needed than external rule. The missionary furnishes the desire and arouses the discontent. The teacher is more powerful than the ruler.

5. CONQUEST AT THE POINT OF THE LANCET.

"China was opened to the gospel at the point of the lancet," said the pioneer, Dr. Peter Parker. "A cure, to their eyes, is the proof of our apostleship," said the veteran Coillard. Dr. Allen was denied op-

*N*ative Medical Staff, Union Medical College, Peking. Illustrates the making of a native medical profession.

*D*ormitory, Union Medical College, Peking. Illustrates Christian union in the social work of missions.

portunities to work for Korea until, when the crown prince had been wounded in a street riot, and the native physicians had failed to stop the flowing blood by stuffing in wax, he was called on as a last resort. He soon mended the torn artery, and from that day was given free scope for his work of healing both body and soul. After Dr. Mackenzie had cured the wife of Li Hung Chang, the port of Tientsin was open to the gospel, and the great viceroy became the friend of Christian benevolence. Dr. Livingstone probed his way through Africa, and was known far and wide in the heart of the Dark Continent as a miracle worker. Dr. Carr won his way into Persia when all others had been denied entrance. Kashmir was a closed land until Dr. Elmslie opened it at the point of his lancet. The story could be repeated on a hundred fields. "The greatest discoveries made in Africa were the roads to the hearts and confidences of the people," said Henry M. Stanley. The medical missionary touches them where they can understand. They know of their physical wounds and diseases, but are often benumbed and unconscious of their moral troubles. The missionary's benevolence in dispensary, hospital, orphanage, school, and by personal friendship not only interprets to them the real heart of the religion of Jesus, but makes them "potent forces, which are to-day influencing and winning the millions of the Far East to the realities and beneficent blessings of a new life," says Wm. Remfry Hunt in "Heathenism Under the Searchlight." John W. Foster, ex-Secretary of State, and noted diplomat, found in surgery "a ready means of overcoming prejudice and opposition."

Opium smokers have been rescued to become effective workers. It is not easy to cure the opium habit. It is said that some of the older officials of China died in their efforts to obey the anti-opium edict. The physicians say that cures are seldom permanent if there be not a mighty purpose in the heart, such as only religion can be trusted to supply. So the faith becomes a part of the materia medica of the good physicians. Evangelist Shi is a notable example of an opium smoker made over into a winner of men. He was a great story teller, and, as is customary in China, related tales to crowds as a sort of monologue dramatist. For twenty years he smoked up his considerable earnings until rescued by Dr. Macklin. For another twenty years he has been an evangelist, with few equals in all China. Not all who come are cured, and not all who are helped become Christians, and not all who become members of the churches are heroes, but the many who are cured commend the religion that sent them such a physician, and the many who are thus led to consider Christianity, and to adopt it, give a testimony that is unanswerable, and from among them come an array of heroic souls that is not equaled outside the mission field. "The aim of foreign missions is not to care for all the industrial, social, economic, and physical ills of the non-Christian world, but to plant there the living seeds of the gospel of the incarnate God," says Robert E. Speer. "The gospel is to be the healing of the World."

Philanthropic work opens the resources of the lands to which it ministers. Buddhism and Confucianism have both been stimulated to imitate the benevolent

134

efforts of Christianity. They have opened schools where before they had none, and Buddhism to-day is copying the Young Men's Christian Association with a Young Men's Buddhist Association. Confucianism's "Halls of Learning" are, in places, taking over the attributes of Association work. The Chinese are building hospitals and endowing them here and there. The only difficulty they meet is that of adequate sympathetic interest on the part of physicians, for the missionary is not equipped with science merely, his sympathy is the better part of the cure. The rich are learning how to give to benevolent enterprises. A Hindu woman recently gave $60,000 for a hospital. Dr. Macklin has received several thousand dollars, one gift being that of $3,000 for his charity work. Li Hung Chang provided for the current expense account of the hospital and dispensary of Dr. Mackenzie at Tientsin, and wealthy Chinese gave $10,000 for its erection. Two years ago the officials at Changsha gave the Yale mission $1,400 for medical work. The late Dowager Empress of China gave $7,500 for the founding of a medical school. The Emperor of Japan gave $5,000 for Young Men's Christian Association work during the Russo-Japanese war. The Crown Prince of Korea gave generously for the Association building in Seoul, as did also Marquis Ito and his friends. These are but few examples. Even in Africa the King of Toro has built a hospital. They might be multiplied innumerably. Some day Christianity will have so leavened the life of the lands to which it takes its message of sympathy and its hand of healing, that they will provide for their own poor and distressed; in doing so it will have lifted the whole earth nearer the Kingdom of God. "The movement led by Christianity has resulted in releasing thousands of the inmates of brothels, in an effective temperance crusade, and in the establishment of many benevolent institutions, such as the famous Ishii orphanage," says John Mott, in speaking of Japan. "The gospel of healing is one that makes its own way into the hearts of the people," said Wu Ting Fang, in commending medical missions. The medical missioner is given entrance into official circles, and all doors open most easily to him. He breaks down prejudice where it counts for most among peoples who are ruled from above and who accept the attitude of the ruler as a model for their own actions in things that relate to the new and the alien. He goes where it would be dangerous for any other man to go, because he takes healing, and all who suffer are grateful to him who gives relief. Thus his lancet opens the door and his message of life is listened unto and becomes a means of ingress to the evangelist and teacher.

The fame of the medical missionary spreads far and wide. He opens hearts by his ministrations, and they open homes by their commendations. Dr. Mackay pulled 21,000 teeth in Formosa, and so relieved a common pain that whole villages were opened to his message. Dr. Macklin was traveling some days from home and where hostility for the foreigner was marked. He could get no entertainment and night was upon them. Mr. Cory, who was with him, was asked, by a man who happened to come along, the usual questions as to where he was from, etc. When he replied "Nankin," the man eagerly asked for Dr. Macklin. When told that he was in the party, this man eagerly invited them into his home, made them comfortable, and hastened to tell the neighbors. Through him many listened that night. He had been cured by the good physician many years before. Mobs have been quieted by such men, and lives saved. They have opened doors long before the evangelist's feet came to enter them. Bars of prejudice and superstition are broken. Dr. Clough baptized 10,000 after his famine relief work, though he had waited long for an opening. Even the most bigoted of Oriental Jews have yielded to the persuasion of the medical missioner. Islamic centers have not been able to deny him entrance, and their fatalism has had to surrender to the magic of his medicine. Among the Mohammedans he must lead the way, for their intolerance is great and all but Moslems are infidels and dogs, but they suffer and are healed, and a friendship thus won opens hearts closed by intolerance and dogmatic hate. Arabia is to-day calling for doctors to open closed doors with their lancets, and there is no place in the world where there is permanent denial to the good physician. His cause runs before him. Dr. Porter received patients from 1,031 different towns and villages. One hospital in Bengal has had patients from 2,091 villages. They come to get personal benefit and go to carry a message of good will to all men. The hospital and the orphanage have arms that reach out to distant places, and voices that speak in many tongues. Their evangel is self-transporting, and they make the voice of the heathen to praise Him who giveth all good. Whole villages are won to the message; entire tribes have been known to turn an open ear and an understanding mind, through the tidings carried by some who had been benefitted by Christian benevolence.

There is no caste in the clinic. The silk-gowned aristocrat sits beside the ragged coolie, for pain makes all men of kin. The missionary refuses to recognize their artificial social lines in his ministrations of healing, whether it is of body or soul. The rich learn a fellow sympathy under his ministrations, and, in gratitude, aid him in the care of the poor. The native Christians become sympathetic and charitable under instruction in the arts of benevolence. The Great Physician commends unto them a spirit of fellow-help, and many become Good Samaritans to the need about them. That parable of neighborliness is often reacted in the mission field, for there the priest passes by the suffering and the despised convert turns aside to lend a hand. Ex-Secretary John Foster said that if not a single convert had been made in the past century, the social and moral benefits that the missionary had taken, in his practical benevolence on the field, would amply pay for all the blood and treasure it had cost. The friendly and sympathetic hand finds way into the closed homes of peoples who condemn their woman-kind to seclusion and ignorance and takes with it cheer and lessons for mind and hand, and above all, a touch of the larger life for the heart of the poor prisoners to a social custom. Here woman carries, as in no other sphere, the sweet sympathy of Christian womanhood.

138

BENEVOLENCE

She takes the sunshine of a new hope inside with her, and not only cures bodies but enlightens eyes, and, in many cases, so breaks down prejudices that doors are opened and a little of the world let in. These ignorant, custom-blinded, and prejudiced women are the main defenders of their own imprisonment and the chief obstacle often in the way of a greater freedom for caste and class. They are superstitious and intolerant of innovation. There are millions of them in Islam and in India and China, who would rather die than allow a male physician touch them. If the husband consents to accept this help, it is only because he is the one in a hundred who loves his wife or daughter enough to throw prejudice to the winds for the sake of saving a life. If he does not so love them he refuses, for wives are cheap and custom is a cruel taskmaster. "We dread your lady doctors," said a Hindu, "they enter our homes, win the hearts of our women, and threaten the foundation of our religion."

Medicine and religion are bound up together in the superstition of heathenism. The witch doctors of savagery are adepts in the arts of incantation, and their theology teaches that suffering is the result of spirit possession. The quackery of all the unscientific practice of paganism is mixed with superstition and religious charlatanry. It is fitting that religion should remedy the superstitious practices of charlatanry and carry a scientific medicament with its intelligence and its liberty for the souls of men. Coming in the name of religion, the treatment is received with a faith that it might not otherwise receive, and the cure opens the way to combat superstition and false religious practices. Above all, it ministers in the name of Him who went about doing good, and so teaches the real art of Christian living as it carries the message of a Christian Savior.

CHAPTER IV

Education: The Means of Progress

1. THE MISSIONARY CONTRIBUTION TO CULTURE.

The conquest of ideas can not be tabulated, but it is none the less sure; it is the undercurrent that irresistibly carries all that floats its seas. The surface play of politics makes for little compared to the deep influence of ideas. Rome conquered Greece politically, but Grecian ideas conquered Rome. The art, the universal language, the philosophy, and the culture of Rome was Grecian. We read the history of the Middle Ages in terms of war and diplomacy, but until we read the history of thought we do not understand that interesting period. We misjudge Christianity when we recount the surface play of ecclesiastical politics during the so-called Dark Ages, and charge it up to the religion of the Nazarene; it was a time of struggle between the political forms and crude customs of the old pagan civilization, and the startling innovations proposed by the new ideas of the Man of Galilee. Those ideas have not yet come into their own, but it is the philosophy of life and the vision of universal brotherhood they bring that is transforming the heart of the world and changing the currents of history.

The missionary has ever been a pioneer in the conquest of ideas. Wherever he has gone he has taken

141

the schoolhouse. He has rooted out idolatry and superstition and banished dark ignorance with the light of his flaming torch. He has given the Scriptures to some five hundred tongues, and is pressing on to give it to all others, and to give with it the universal art of reading. He has written text-books, compiled dictionaries, constructed grammars, translated works of science, law, religion, political economy, history, and sociology, and counted every item of knowledge he could put into the vernacular of a people a distinct contribution to their welfare, and a step in bringing in the Kingdom of God. Robert Morrison not only translated the entire Bible into Chinese, but compiled an encyclopedic dictionary of their difficult language; either task would have been a monumental work for one man. William Carey translated the Scriptures and other religious material into more than thirty languages and dialects in India, and founded a college besides. Gutzlaff wrote sixty-one volumes in Chinese, two in Japanese, one in Siamese, five in Dutch, seven in German, and nine in English. The Chinese have been debtors to the most phenomenal literary labors of modern times. Morrison, besides the monumental labors mentioned above, wrote twenty-five volumes in Chinese, Milne gave them twenty-four, Legge twenty, and Faber twenty-seven, while Dr. Muirhead, in later times, gave them thirty books, Dr. McCartee thirty-four, and Dr. Edkins wrote fourteen in Chinese, seven in English, and one in Mongolian. Other fields have received like contributions in literature, and there is no phase of human knowledge that has not been given to the pagan world at Christian hands and given as a glad contribution for their welfare. One mission press of China puts out 84,000,000 pages annually, and another in India more than 76,000,000 pages. The 160 mission presses in all the fields issue no less than 12,000,000 copies of various publications annually, according to Dr. Dennis, and send out more than 400,000,000 pages as Sibylline leaves to carry prophecy of the coming better day, when the knowledge of the Lord shall cover the earth as the waters the sea. Bibles and parts of the Bible are annually distributed by hundreds of thousands, and in all the older missionary fields are now gladly purchased by the people. This general diffusion of knowledge among the reading minority has stimulated greatly the love of learning among all the people, and substituted a live and modern view of the world for the ancient traditions. It has vastly aided China, Japan, and Korea to turn their faces from the sunset of the past to the sunrise of the future. It is helping to put a historical perspective back of Hindu speculation, and to train the Indian mind toward practical and serviceable knowledge. The missionary sets ideas to work, and, increasing modern knowledge, banishes ancient superstitions, and turns the pagan mind from its distorted conception of natural phenomena to a more scientific conception of nature, and thus sets him on the road to open-mindedness and progress.

When the first Irish missionaries set out on their journeys to the wild men of Scotland, Northumbria, Friesland, and Germany, they took with them the fundamentals of education. In Ireland, St. Patrick's Christian settlements had been communities for instruction. Columba founded a school with his church at Iona. Boniface's monasteries in Germany were also schools. The Jesuits originated the idea of separate Christian communities in their "Reductions" in Paraguay, and carried the idea into the missions of California; in them they taught the converts the rudiments of learning and gave an industrial training. Duff became the founder of the modern school system in India. Verbeck established the first college in Japan, and is the real founder of the Imperial University. Dr. Murray was invited from America by the Japanese Government to establish its modern school system. Dr. Martin has been justly called the father of modern education in China. Stewart, of Lovedale, set the type of educational institution for savage Africa, the inspector of schools for South Africa saying, "A visit to Lovedale would convert the greatest skeptic regarding the value of native education." The missionary is the real founder of modern education in all the non-Christian lands. He sows the seed, sets the ideal, inspires the organization, and generally manages the beginnings of governmental efforts, besides actually educating the leaders in his own institutions.

The non-Christian world is an ignorant world. Two-thirds of humanity can not read and write, and the most of that illiterate population is non-Christian. In India there are 278,000,000 illiterates, or 891 to the thousand, while in the United States there are only 65 to the thousand. In Japan only the upper classes could read and write before Western civilization entered. All Africa is black and sodden in ignorance, and, except where the missionary has taught them, do not so much as know that writing is possible. China has long honored her literati, but has had no public school system that reached the masses, and has left her womankind in almost total ignorance. Korea's education began within the missionary era of her present inner transformation. Confucianism and Brahmanism both possess educational ideas, but both make it the vehicle for turning the face to the past, and crystalize social custom and forbid progress. Confucianism is democratic in that it opens the way for any boy to become learned if his parents can purchase the instruction, but it provides no universal education and it instructs in the classics instead of the sciences, and trains the mind by verbal memory rather than in logical thinking. Its classical writings are morally pure, even more so than those of the ancients we teach to our Western youth, and they, at least, are set into the circle of the national life, but they give little practical knowledge, and they bound China to the mummies of a past. Brahmanism forbids instruction to any but the caste, and thus denies education her right to remake society; she makes learning consist in subtle speculation and knows no practical arts. Buddhism is the most liberal and progressive of the non-Christian faiths, but even she has never reared a public school system, made learning popular, or educated women, and her desire to escape from the toil of things material destroys all desire to know more of the practical world. In Burma, Siam, and Tibet, where Buddhism has been kept purest and has been regnant for centuries, she has never educated the populace. Islam led the world in the gift of culture for four centuries, but had no power to overcome her own limitations, and her world to-day is one of blind ignorance, fatalism, and superstition.

The East is awakening to the advantages of education. They have discovered there is no hope of progress except through the school as the vehicle. There are 500,000 youth in the high schools, colleges, and universities of Asia to-day. One-fifth of all of them are in the missionary institutions for higher learning; this measures somewhat the part the missionary is playing in the educational renaissance of the East. But no government, with the single exception of Japan, has yet arisen to the situation and furnished adequate instruction for all. In China the most remarkable transformation in the history of the world is taking place. Her temples are being turned into schoolhouses, and her ancient examination stalls have been torn down in favor of modern learning and more approved and efficient civil service equipment. Her officials have urged the people to give their offering for the dead to the schools; it would amount in Shanghai alone to $350,000 annually. In Tientsin the government has forbidden such gifts and has established modern schools from primary to university. Her projected educational system will establish a university in every province, a high school in every considerable town, an elementary school in every village, and crown all with magnificent graduate and technical universities. But to-day she is able to furnish schooling to only one in from every forty to fifty-five of her youth, and has as yet only a few of the million teachers it will take to instruct all her young people.

Ajmer College, North India. The athletic ground and school buildings here shown illustrate the full-rounded type of education given in the mission school. The mission boys always stand high and usually win in contests. Due to clean living.

EDUCATION

In India, with the English Government's universal school system, there is only one in every fifty-seven under instruction, and the missionaries are educating one-third of all who attend college. In all the non-Christian world not more than one-tenth of the population can find a school open for their children, and of that tenth the great mass are not inspired with a desire for education. Tradition surrenders slowly, except it be given a mighty dynamic within.

The missionaries are to-day instructing nearly 1,500,000 youth in their 25,000 institutions of learning. Some of the large institutions of higher learning are under missionary auspices. In India they have 72 high schools, colleges, and universities with more than 250 students each, and there are 17 colleges with a total attendance of more than 17,000 students, several of them with from 1,400 to 1,800 apiece. St. Peter's College at Tanjore, Madras, has educated more than 5,000 young men; Assiut College, in Egypt, has graduated 2,000, and St. John's, in Rangoon, Burmah, has taught more than 12,000. The United Presbyterian mission in Egypt conducts 150 schools, with an attendance of 16,000 students, one-fourth of whom are Moslems. In Persia there are 5,000 in the mission schools, and in some of them one-half the pupils are Moslems. The Syrian Protestant College at Beirut, Syria, has 850 students and a faculty of seventy-two men; it is making the leaders for all that territory and is finely equipped. Robert College at Constantinople is one of the most remarkable of existing educational institutions. Prof. William Ramsey says he found their graduates over all Turkey and the Balkans, and that everywhere they are men of integrity, patriotism, and breadth of culture. It was the graduates of Roberts that led in the emancipation of Bulgaria. Urumia College bids fair to become to Persia what Roberts has been to the Balkans and Turkey. In all Turkey there are 700 schools, with 41,000 students, largely under Congregational auspices, and they have furnished the new blood and the modern ideas, in no small part, for the remaking of the empire. In Japan the missionaries are now confining their educational work to that which the government does not adequately supply, *i. e.*, kindergartens and high schools. The Doshisha was the pioneer of Christian schools there and graduated many of the leaders of modern Japan. Its alumni have recently raised $100,000 for its further endowment. St. John's College in Shanghai is one of the solidest educational institutions in all the East. Madras University is a great school, with over 1,700 students. In Africa the Blantyre Mission has fifty-seven schools, with 4,000 pupils, and the Livingstone Mission has 207 schools, with 16,000 students. In Uganda there are 60,000 under instruction, and it is a disgrace not to be able to read. These are but a few of the large number that might be named.

Some of the great student centers of the world are now to be found in the Eastern capitals. Tokio claims first place, with 50,000, while Calcutta has 20,000, Peking has 17,000, and Cairo has more than 10,000. The tendency is for the masses of students to gather in these centers in each country. The great question of the day is regarding the moral quality that

these students will take away from the colleges with
them. Herbert Spencer said, "The idea that mere
education is a panacea for political evils is a delusion."
He was introduced at a dinner given him by the notable
literary men and educators of New York by William
M. Evarts, who, as toastmaster, said, out of compliment
to the great compiler and apostle of knowledge, that
the attainment and diffusion of knowledge was the
promise and the hope of America. He replied that
he was embarrassed to have to take issue with one
who had given him so kindly an introduction, but
that it was not knowledge but character that was the
hope and promise of America. Premier Katsura, of
Japan, wrote President Harada, of the Doshisha University, congratulating him upon the manner in which
the college had stamped character upon the young men
of Japan, and said, "May it become a citadel of culture." In India even the government officials acknowledge the inefficiency of the national schools in the
training of character. Count Okuma has been especially emphatic in his apostleship of the idea that
character must be given with education or it is a failure,
and has ever commended both the Christian schools
and Christian ethics as the true source of it. The
school of a non-Christian land does not have the Christian for a teacher as it usually does in America and
Britain, and education all too often means no social
conscience, but only a means for individual preferment.
As a consequence, the educated man is not less licentious or corrupt in office, but more artful, and,
without social conscience, he fails to uplift his kind.
"What you would put into the life of a nation, put

into its schools," says an old German proverb. All the East is awakening to the need of a high moral tone in education. One-half of the 100,000 young men in the higher schools of learning conducted by the missionaries will give themselves to teaching.

2. CREATING A LEADERSHIP.

The Christian community becomes a leaven in the midst of the pagan community; its ideals gradually take hold, and many who do not confess the faith come to practice the precept. Keshub Chunder Sen, the founder of the Brahmo Somaj of India, was led by the teachings of Christianity. Mozoomdar was converted by Christianity, and, while unable to unite with a divided church, gave his great influence to Christian morals. Many of the leaders of Japan and China have accepted the morals of Christianity and plead with their youth to do the same. The late progressive king of Siam was educated by a missionary. But it is not the leaders alone who are lifted up by contact with Christian thought; it enters into the customs of the common people and raises the standards of living and the grade of common intelligence. There is no influence so pervasive as that of personal contact, and every true native Christian touches many of his neighbors. Thus there comes a leadership of ideals and ideas that is pervasive and elevates all living.

Nothing more fatal could happen than for a people to accept the externals of Christianity without getting its vital life. They would have thrown away what discipline their old faith gave them, and taken none of the moral sanctions of the new in its stead. Here

150

lies the danger of Western innovation and material advantage impinging upon the culture of the East and the barbarous life of savagery. Education assimilates the outward to the inner and fits a man to enjoy the greater material advantages of civilization and freedom from the old bondage, without losing himself in a riot of riches that he does not know how to use. "A change of mind is needed as well as a change of heart." Mere conversion is not enough; the convert must be instructed in the things of the new life. The danger of education in Asia is that it will fail to give character to the leaders of the next generation. The destruction of the old superstition is followed by a reaction against religion. Such was the case in Japan, where a smattering of scientific knowledge all too often meant the danger of a little learning. Most of the 40,000 students in the higher government schools of learning in India are skeptics in regard to all religion. No educated man is an idolater, and all too often he is a materialist, pure and simple. It is fortunate for India that every third college man is under Christian instruction.

Missions have played one of their greatest rôles in the furnishing of leadership for the awakened nations of the East. William Elliot Griffis says that previous to 1890 most of the leaders of new Japan had been educated in the mission schools; that fact may account for the lack of excesses in the revolution. One-half the mission students of China take up teaching or direct Christian service, and their influence in tempering the new era will be recognized by the leaders of new China. In Japan no less than twenty of the editors of the leading dailies are Christian men, while the number of Christians in Parliament and the leading offices of state is out of all proportion to the number of church members in the empire. Duff said, "The real reformers of Hindustan will be the well qualified Hindus." The Director of Public Instruction for India said, twenty years ago, that at the present rate the Christian community of India would ultimately furnish most of the professional leadership of the nation, and that they bid fair to become the industrial leaders as well. An instance of their progress in leadership in China is given by the Commercial Press of Shanghai. It was organized by Christian young men, graduates of mission schools, and took for its avowed purpose the creation of a Christian enterprise on Christian principles, and was inspired by the opportunity to serve the nation through furnishing good literature. To-day it does a business of a million a year, furnishes 70% of all the books printed in China, keeps the Lord's Day, and is one of the most reputable and honorable business enterprises to be found anywhere. The literature of modern Japan is predominantly from the hands of men educated in the mission schools.

If the church is to be strong on the mission field, it must have an educated leadership, and that leadership must be increasingly native. No foreigner can appeal to a people as can their own leaders. Those missions that have paid all but exclusive attention to evangelism and have neglected education are to-day suffering for leadership, while those that both evangelized and educated are growing with increasing momentum. The London Missionary Society is notable among the latter; it is to-day multiplying its native staff much more rapidly than that of its foreign leaders, and reaping consequent benefits in self-supporting churches, Christianized communities, and an efficient public leadership for all social advancement. In Japan 15% of the graduates of mission colleges have gone into teaching or direct Christian service, 5% have taken government positions, 30% have gone into business and the professions, while 35% are pursuing advanced studies. In China the mission student is handicapped at present by governmental regulation. China is yet afraid lest foreign instruction means the domination of the alien, and compels all government students to bow to the tablet of Confucius and forbids any to vote who are not from government schools. These fears will soon subside, and, as in Japan, the Christian young men of education will exert a wide influence in the making of the new China. There is also a great handicap to the Chinese church in its claims on its graduates for direct Christian service. They are accused tauntingly of "eating the foreigner's rice," are compelled to work for from one-third to one-twentieth what commercial and government service pays, and, in some instances, ignorantly classed with the priestly element and despised accordingly. That one-half enter either direct Christian service or teaching, and thus become the real leaven of the new order, is a magnificent tribute to their spirit of self-sacrifice and their love of fellow-man. The new patriotism in China exalts service of the nation to an almost religious enthusiasm, but the missionary is even less concerned about making officials than he is

SOCIAL WORK OF CHRISTIAN MISSIONS

about furnishing the educators and social welfore exponents of the new era; for the men who create the ideals and inculcate the ideas for the new era will most effectually mould it. The church in every mission field needs men who will interpret Christian principles into the indigenous thought of the people. To that end the missionary candidates of to-day should be well instructed in pedagogy, and know how to impress the mind of the native student with principles without destroying his personality as a native. The mission school is vastly superior to any other on the field, in both morals and pedagogical efficiency, but the latter needs further strengthening. Most of the higher schools of learning are sadly undermanned. What they are able to do with their inadequate staffs is one of the marvels of missions, but if the church would rise to her opportunities, she will supply adequate faculties and hasten the day when Christianity will have both a competent leadership for herself in the field, and also multiply her power to furnish thoroughly Christianized leaders for all spheres of life.

Educated youth make the morrow. In our own country the 1% that takes a full college course occupy 70% of the positions of influence. How much more will it be so in nations in the making? The education of the many lifts immeasurably the whole standard of living. The missionary generally has to begin with the lower classes in his schools as in his churches, but education makes these dispossessed of one generation the leaders of the next. Efficiency will eventually take command, even though the odds be great. The educational ideal of life leavens the whole social life of a people. It establishes a democracy and destroys caste. In India to-day there are 170,000,000 bound by the thongs of caste. In all paganism womankind is socially of lower caste. Most religions stand for a sort of caste preferment for their adherents. Mohammedanism constitutes itself a proud caste wherever it exists. Brahmanism confines its glories to the few who are born within its sacred precincts. Those educated in the writings of Confucius are a select class in China. A Brahman of note said before an audience in Allahabad, "I am a Brahman of the Brahmans, and of the most orthodox school, but I must confess that the way in which Christianity has raised the Pariahs of Madras is beyond all praise and puts me to shame as a Hindu." The Christian patriot of Madras says, "The Christians look back to the era when a few Galilean peasants turned the world upside down and shook the ancient fabric of civilization, and then look forward to when the emancipated Pariah shall stand amongst those redeemed by Christ from every kindred, and tongue, and people, and nation." Idleness is no longer dignified, work becomes respectable, and it is no longer said as in a Hindu proverb, "He who reads must be waited upon by him who does not." Self-reliance and confidence take hold of the lowly and men are made potential with a new power. A new environment is gradually created, and in it the multitudes who follow are given a larger opportunity. "It must be remembered," said Gladstone, "that the moral standards of individuals are fixed, not alone by their personal convictions, but by the principles, the traditions, and the habits of the society

155

in which they live and below which it is a point of honor, as well as of duty, not to sink. A religious system is only, then, truly tested when it is set to reform and to train, on a territory of its own, great masses of mankind." With this challenge, Christianity goes to educate the leadership of the nations, confident that what has come to pass in the West will also come to pass in the East, and unto the uttermost parts of the earth in the course of time, and that all men will be elevated into high planes of a civilized life as the leaven of knowledge and of righteousness runs through the whole measure.

3. TURNING LIABILITIES INTO ASSETS.

"As a pagan, the Indian was a liability; as a Christian he is becoming an increasing asset," says a Canadian Government Blue Book. Practically all missionary work among the Indians has been conducted with industrial training. The success of Metlakahtla, and such superbly successful efforts to create a higher type of Indian community, has been based upon the training of hand with head and heart. William Duncan has made Metlakahtla a type of peace and prosperity, such as few pioneer white communities can show. He found the Tsimshian Indians of British Columbia a savage, degraded tribe. They gave him scant courtesy and put him in grave danger often. After a patient effort he won their confidence, induced them to give up drunkenness, and organized them into an industrial community. It became a model of peaceful, industrious, Christian neighborliness, and is to-day one of the shining examples of missionary

A Class in Carpentry—Rhodesia, Africa. Illustrating the practical manner in which the mission school founds education in the practical arts.

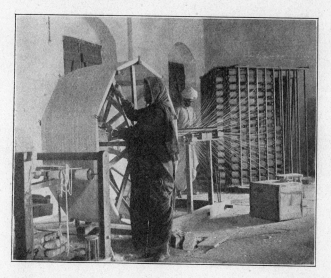

Cotton Weaving in India, illustrating how the missionary helps the people to help themselves.

power to create a civilization. The primitive man has little sense of precision or accuracy, and less of logical thinking. The watch and the mirror excite his wonder, if indeed they do not arouse his apprehension lest they be possessed of demons; but it never occurs to him to make inquiries as to their construction until the white man gives him the lesson that unburdens his conception of magic and instills the first ideas of science. In the native mind, idea and action are not always coupled together. The reality of a thing and the thought concerning it are not connected. The Hindu may possess the finest of speculative intellects, but he can not invent a harvesting machine; so, too, he may know all the doctrine and not think of his obligation to live it. Character consists not in knowledge, but in doing what one knows to do. Stewart, of Lovedale, said that the native "confounds instruction and education." He may learn all the lessons, but not practice any of them. What he learns must be assimilated into character and personality. He must be not a hearer only, but a sincere doer of the word.

The catch-word of present-day pedagogy is, "no impression without expression." It is dangerous to know much and to feel much without doing much. It is of such stuff that hypocrites are made. The missionary finds a people in Africa and other barbarous lands that are idle and without ambition. In the Malay States it is impossible to hire the natives to work. A shake of the tree and he has fruit, a line into the sea and he has fish, a bit of beaten bark and his wife has him a garment; he builds his house of a few bamboo, and may while the sultry days away with

games and the chewing of beetle-nut, so why should
he work; money would only buy things he does not
need, and he has no ambition to raise his standard
of life. In contrast to this is the report from the
interior of Africa, where Dr. Laws of the Livingstonia
Mission tells of thousands of formerly idle, half-
starved Tongas now in the employ of the African
Lakes Co., and even of hundreds of the wild and warlike Angoni, formerly contemptuous of aught but the
raid and bloodshed, having become industrious and
peaceable in their habits, all through industrial training in that mission. The Catholic Bishop, Casar-
telli, says that their experience in North Africa is, "that
without some preliminary training in habits of work
and industry, which are at least the rudiments of
civilization, religious or moral teaching has little if
any moral effect." It trains the constructive or creative powers and develops faculties that book instruction does not develop; it stimulates the motor activities
and cultivates the inventive faculties; it gives resourcefulness and a sense of possession that arouses
the instincts for accumulation, without which man
will not provide for the morrow. "The native thinks
little of the future," says the Principal of Blytheswood.
It is a feast or a famine with him. He gets a regard
for work, whereas he has despised it. The luxury of
idleness is an ideal of savagery. Industrial instruction
trains his mind in observation, precision, accuracy,
and creation; it panoplies him with those fundamentals
of civilization—thrift, industry, and a desire to do
things. There is an economic basis of civilization.
The pagan peoples are poverty-stricken because they

158

have so little creative power and because they have little idea of conservation.

Civilization arouses new wants. The artisan is necessary to progress. The native must begin where he is, and build step at a time. He can not lift himself with book education if it makes him abhor his kind, or does not fit him to do the next best thing for his people. The Livingstonia Mission in Central Africa gives its industrial instruction in houses built of the same material its students will have to use in their future work in the village. It aims to use the native tools and such improvements on them as can be made, together with instruments that the native-trained artisan can make for himself, in order that he may not be a workman without tools. European tools are better, but they are expensive and remote, and the aim is to make all skill acquired practicable to the immediate situation in Central Africa. Some missions have erred in training lads to become skilled in things that were not in demand in their country, and thus left them skilled but without a job. Hampton and Tuskegee furnish the models for modern industrial mission schools. Their ideal is to fit the student to meet the actual conditions as they exist about him, and to better them in all practical ways; to make every graduate capable of earning a livelihood for himself and family, among his own people and by ministering to their welfare, and to give every one a desire to do actual labor. The first pupils in the African missions were taunted by the proud idlers, who lived by the work of their wives, with "selling their skins for money;" but the brigand was turned into an honest worker and industry replaced the slave raid. The native hut was built higher and wider and the new economic factor put on clothing in place of his old war paint and tattooing. The crooked path that had been made by generations of savage feet was broadened into a roadway, and oxen were hitched to the loads that women and bare-backed men had been accustomed to carry.

A literary training may "make drones where workers are needed." It is a missionary experience that the native may be educated out of his environment by being taught as the American school teaches. There must ever be teachers, preachers, and clerical workers trained, but even they will be all the better trained by having wholesome education in the arts and crafts. The old Jewish custom would be good for the latest civilization. Every person would do well to have a trade, and if there be any truth in John Ruskin's idea that there was no guarantee of wholesome character except one had toiled with his hands, it is dangerous to not have been through the discipline of industrial labor. The native who is sent abroad is liable to return with a contempt for his lowly brethren, and to be so educated above their manner of life that he can not articulate with it sufficiently to help them.

The late Charles Cuthbert Hall was convinced that industrial training was as beneficial as either evangelistic or medical missions in India. The Hindu has some arts that are rare, but in the best of them he uses the most primitive methods and wastes untold strength. The practical arts are not well developed, and the resources of the land and the people are not more than touched. The government is doing much to develop material resources, but until the people are made resourceful the greatest mine of livelihood is untouched. The native convert is liable to be ostracized and cast out, both from the common fund of his family and from the trade in which his guild works. The industrial school makes him self-supporting and self-reliant, and builds up a self-sustaining Christian community. The orphan children would be mere beggars and parasites on society if they were trained in mind and not in hand as well. The government schools have educated so many for clerical positions that desks are overcrowded; the great need of the land is for practical workers who can build up the solid foundations of life in character and economic resourcefulness, and break down the paralyzing system of caste that lays its hand on industry, as well as on all social life. In China the people are industrious, perhaps the most hard-working people in the world, but they use the tools of the times of Abraham. Their farms are tilled with a stick, sharpened with a flat piece of iron, a club hoe, and a hook that serves for reaper and general utility instrument. In the African industrial missions the steel plowshare was introduced and literally thousands of them have been adopted. "Why, they do the work of ten women," said the wondering natives. Chinese industries need modernization, and the adaptation of modern arts to native thrift puts the native Christian to the fore as a leader in his community. Dr. Osgood tells how he led a native carpenter into the better way through

11   161

the use of a brace and bit. The appalling poverty and the barren hardness of daily living among China's millions is due, not to lack of native resources, but to lack of native resourcefulness. China can not build an enduring civilization of the new order without a solid foundation in the industrial arts and a rise in the standard of life among her masses. When the missionary trains the hands he trains in character and makes the individual able to lift his share in the betterment of society. Industrial missions do not play the part in China that they do in Africa, or even in India, but they have a large part to play in the educational work of the missionary. In Japan the thorough modernization of all life leaves the industrial mission pretty much the same function that it plays in education at home. The missionary has found it very necessary and useful in the orphanage, and wherever he offers any schooling in the common grades it becomes an integral part of good instruction. In Africa the industrial mission is the true foundation of all education and progress. When Dr. James Stewart proposed that the most fitting memorial to David Livingstone was a mission that would instruct the natives in the foundations of industrial order and usefulness and make Christians of them, he solved Africa's educational problem. The solution now only needs pushing on to the limits of its possibilities, and to the shores of the continent. Blantyre, Lovedale, Blytheswood, Livingstonia, and many others, are giving the example. It is safe to say that there is practically no mission in all Africa that does not use the industrial method, and in them tens of thousands are receiving,

or will receive, the foundations for a new and better
era. Civilization arouses new wants, and the missionary fails if he does not put into the hands of the
new disciple the means of supplying them. In Central
Africa there is a settlement of native Chrsitians that
has carved out a community life by the arts of their
hands and through the desires of their Christianized
hearts. A few of them first went off into the woods
alone, and others were welcomed as they came. It is
a place of peace and order, and even the Moslems have
been coming to share in the new and better way. In
India Christian communities of Pariahs have been
established, and the poor outcast has become a self-
respecting freeman, worthy, industrious, and self-
supporting, under his own initiative.

4. TEACHING THE MOTHERS OF THE RACE.

"Since the world began it was never known that
a woman could read," said the people of South India,
when the first school for girls was opened. The non-
Christian world has no system of instruction for its
womankind. One of the most startling innovations
of the missionary was the school for girls. The Hindu
said, "You had as well try to teach the monkeys to
read;" the Moslem said the same, only used the mule
for his comparison. The savage marveled that the
missionary talked and ate with his wife and made the
ox do her work. England opened schools for India
in 1854, but in that sad land only one out of two-
hundred women above twenty-five years of age can
read or write. In China not more than one woman
out of three-thousand can read or write. In Japan

the modern educational system is educating the girls, but takes few above what we know as the "common school" grades. The government provides no universities for women, and the three normal schools it does support cut off one year from the work given men. There is a great university for women in Tokio, with 1,000 students, but it was founded and is managed by a Christian scholar. In India the Hindu girls go to school, if at all, only until they are about eleven or twelve years old; they are then taken out to be married. There is only one girl out of every five hundred students in the high schools, and of the 112 women in the arts colleges, forty-three are Christians and thirty-three Parsis. In the primary grades the girls furnish only one pupil in seventeen, and only four out of every thousand of school age attend school at all; in the Central Provinces even that number must be divided by two. In comparison with America, only one Hindu girl goes to school to every seven hundred of our daughters.

In all pagan lands the women are the citadels of religious superstition; their ignorance and prejudice and natural religious interests make them such. The conservative men of pagan lands fear the education of their women as no other modern innovation. It means the overthrow of their ancient prerogatives of absolute lordship and a readjustment of the family life that spells revolution to the social order. Woman is an inferior creature, and all creation will be overthrown if she be not kept such. Hinduism and Buddhism teach that she has no salvation except she be born again as man; education teaches her that there

164

is a worth in her own soul. The Chinese women replied to early missionaries that it was no use to teach them, they had no souls. Even Burman women, the freest of all, have little education, though they possess an initiative that makes them superior to their husbands in much, and, when educated in Christian schools, acquire a grace and poise that makes them the equal of their Western sisters. There is no elevation of race possible, unless its mothers are elevated; one had as well expect water to rise above its own sources. Woman becomes the citadel of religious morality once she is Christian; the natural refinements of her nature and the mother instinct for the preservation of her young make her so. "There is not a woman in Christendom that is not under infinite obligations to the Christ," says A. McLean. If women were sensitive to the benefits that Christianity confers upon their sex, they would not only outnumber the men in the churches, they would so train their sons in the love of Christianity, for their mother's sake, that multitudes more of them would pay a juster tribute of respect to the emancipator of their mothers.

When Mrs. Marshman founded the first school for women in India more than a century ago, she drove the thin end of the wedge into the bed rock of heathenism. India has produced some of the most remarkable women of the last and present generations; but every one of them has been educated in mission schools, or has come under the influence of missionaries. "For a woman to be without ability is her virtue," was a Chinese proverb, but a Chinese woman's journal to-day declares, "The woman who remains in ignorance wrongs not only herself, but her family and her country." "What women these Christians have," cried the teacher of Chrysostom of old, and Mozoomdar wrote the same back to India when he attended the Congress of Religions in Chicago. In Cairo there was recently held a great mass meeting of women at which a princess made the leading address. They demanded that the harem be overthrown, the veil discarded, and that they have the right to give their own hands in wedlock. The schools for girls have not wrought in vain in Egypt; even men who were bitterly opposed to them now desire their graduates as wives for their sons. The Moslem girls of Syria were formerly married at the age of twelve, but the Christian school has so wrought among them that few are now married before fifteen, while the Christian girls wait until they are eighteen or twenty; thus is given another concrete instance of the social leaven at work in the mass, through the influence of a minority who are under thralldom to the principles of the gospel. In Siam the Minister of Education said that it was through the influence of missionary schools, and the work of Christian women in teaching girls, that schools for them were founded in Siam and supported by the government. In Korea the rapidly growing Christian community can not get enough teachers to instruct all their children; for the new found faith opens their natural hearts, and they desire all their children educated without reference to sex. In China one-half of the Christian women learn to read, though they are not converted until mature. "Your Bible must have been written by a woman," said one of them, "it says so many kind things about women." The missionary does not confine his instruction to the school room; the church itself becomes a school and the lesson is carried into the home itself by the hands of those faithful women who do the effective evangelism of home visitation. Mrs. Montgomery says the "woman's club" seems to follow Christianity all over the earth and tells of one in Portuguese West Africa, to which scores of the native women come, some walking as much as one hundred miles to attend. They talk over all those home problems that women in our own land talk over when they come together in their mothers' meetings, and no more effective civilizing work could be done than that of guiding their minds in the discovery of humane ways of caring for their children, and in teaching them that cleanliness which is next to Godliness.

The education that is given on the mission field must be of the practical sort which fits the pupil to live in the midst of her native surroundings, and to grapple with local problems. The missionary does not build a great church edifice after the type of modern Western architecture, and stand up in it to preach to a people who have never learned what a church edifice is; he begins at their hearts and leads them along the upward way until he can lead them into the church which they may build with their own hands. So the education of heathen women must begin with their own problems and possibilities; to educate them out of their environment would be to waste time and lose opportunity as well as to make miserable the victims of mistaken method. It is no use to cry out against the position in which she is placed and butt the head of idealism against the stone wall of immemorial custom. It is better to overthrow it by the disintegrating force of new ideals in the native mind. The prejudice against woman becoming a public personage was respected by Paul when he counseled the women of Corinth to wear their veils. The women of Turkey took the same counsel to themselves, in the larger interests of reform, and resumed the veils they threw off when freedom first came. They will all the more surely be able to put them off in the end. The native ideals of woman's place in the home furnish the best channels for operation, and to make her a better homekeeper and a companion of her husband, to compel his respect for her and give her ability to rear her children with competence, is to put dynamite under the granite walls of pagan custom. An educated womanhood means the end of concubinage and polygamy and the gradual attainment of her right to refuse her hand in wedlock. Paganism makes her either a drudge or a toy. The first schools for the daughters of nobility and for the higher castes found parents unwilling that the girls should be taught domestic arts; they were to be the toys of rich men. The school brought a new idea of her place as a responsible factor in home life, and raised her from the position of a beautifully feathered bird in the cage to that of a mature and responsible wife and mother. These women are now founding schools for their own sex, such as Miss Tsuda's in Tokio, and Ramabai's in Poona, and are editing journals advocating the freedom of their kind. In Peking, a Mrs. Chang edits a woman's daily, devoted to all the reforms that the most progressive Chinese women desire. There must be highly educated leaders who can lead the minds of their sisters and do the work of teachers and physicians, but the masses of women must make homes, and the missionary seeks to make of them such home-keepers that the homes will be the transforming places of a new generation. There are not enough of the former as yet, and it is good missionary policy to train a host of native women to lead their kind into the higher life, for the most benign foreign Christian can not so search the heart of a people as can one of their own race.

5. EDUCATION AS AN EVANGELIZING AGENCY.

"When the infant goes to school, his father will soon follow him to church," said a French missionary. The kindergarten and primary school have been the fruitful source of many conversions to Christianity. They have trained up a generation of children with respect for the faith and with minds well filled with the ideals of Christ, and they have opened the understanding and won the hearts of many parents. Among the Karens 60% of the present-day members of the church were won through the schools. Eugene Stock, head of the great Church Missionary Society, and one of the greatest authorities on missions, says that in India the schools conducted by the missionaries have brought a greater number into the church than all other agencies combined. In Japan high school instruction has proved the most fertile evangelistic field. The age of adolescence is the fruitful period for reaping religious convictions. Missions would do well to make all possible of this stage of instruction. The churches at home are learning from modern psychology that adolescence, or the high-school age of youth, is the time of life when ideals reign most supremely in the mind, and when young men and women put their instruction into action most readily. They are casting off from the moorings of paternal authority and turning out into the seas of self-reliance and independent action; it is the revolutionary period of life, the turning time. A thousand high and middle schools in China to-day would reap a mature fruitage of educated and self-reliant men for the service of the cause to-morrow. The Doshisha students are under such educational management as are the students of Yale and Columbia, *i. e.*, the school is Christian but not denominational, and is conducted for the purposes of a broad education and not for that of conversion, yet the influence is such that one-third of all are baptized before they finish their course. This is really a remarkable record when we consider that the students come so largely from Buddhist homes, and from parents who, howsoever much they may be adapting their lives to the Christian way of thinking, do not consider that it is at all necessary or possible for them to unite with the infant church. In some of the mission schools of Japan as high as 65% of the pupils and 95% of the graduates become Christians. In all fields there have been more conversions among the educated classes during the past decade than ever before. Through the schools, the Christian theory of things, and the whole body of Christian history

EDUCATION

and philosophy is getting into the minds of the people, and all are drawn nearer the Christian conception of life. Christianity is no longer a strange and despised religion because of its being a faith not comprehended. In Livingstonia one-half the church members are the direct product of the schools. The evangelist may sow the best of seed in unprepared soil, and it may be unable to root deeply into life for the very lack of a prepared heart. Evangelism, as conducted on the mission field, is a matter of instruction; the preacher teaches, and before he baptizes his inquirer he examines him closely. But many can not hear because their ears are deafened with the discordant voices of old superstitions, and their hearts are hardened with vice.

Education is almost the only way of reaching the high castes and the Moslems. Duff founded his college because of this fact. He found the proud Brahman inaccessible to preaching but a possible student under the tender of mature instruction, for he is an educated man and honors learning. The same thing is true of the literati of China. The Samurai of Japan have been the most fruitful class for the effective evangel of education. Their devotion to learning led them to the mission school, and as they turned their backs upon the past they opened their minds to the mature lesson of Christianity. The Moslem man is supposed to read the Koran; it is a religious duty. He may be uneducated but be able to pick out the Arabic of his sacred book. In Nigeria it was found that natives who knew not a word of Arabic were so drilled that they could pronounce the words of the Koran, though they knew not what one of them meant. But education destroys the Koran. Literary criticism pulls down its every citadel of authority as it does that of the sacred books of India, stripping them of the husks of myth, legend, and puerility, to say nothing of the unspeakable impurities there is in them—so impure that the English government in India forbade the printing of English translations of some of them. The contradictions, fatalism, superstitions, and gross materialism of the Koran are revealed to the educated Moslem, and, while he may keep a form of fealty to it, he will not be longer a fanatical and intolerant worshiper of its very covers. His mind is broadened, his old intolerance broken down, his prejudices replaced by ideas, he imbibes the spirit of Christian charity and becomes a new type of folk in the midst of Moslem society. To wear down the fanaticism of Islam, to give the Mohammedan world a fairer view of the Christian world after thirteen centuries of conflict, to put the spirit of the old Crusaders behind the gospel of the love of Christ, is the best that can be hoped for in the present, perhaps, but it is none the less a true evangelism, for it is preparing for a time when conversions will come by the thousands. There are to-day some 5,000 Moslem students in mission schools. Not many of them will actually join the church, the prejudice is yet so great, and the fanaticisn that lingers is sufficient to forbid instruction in Christian history and doctrine, though it is given in some schools, but all of them will be nearer the goal and they will make a new generation of open minds.

172

The First Class of Christian Inquirers in Tibet. Dr. Shelton and Mr. Ogden baptized the first Christians in that land from this number.

Advanced Class in Urumia College, Persia. Moslems, Jews, and Christians are here drawn together, and ancient hates are lost under missionary instruction.

EDUCATION

Education is an evangelism of preparation where it does not directly bring the pupil into the church. It cultivates soil for the sowing even where the seed of direct Christian fealty does not take root. A noted English evangelist conducted a successful campaign among the missions of Ceylon, but found that nearly every one of his converts had been in the mission schools. The new can not always effectively enter until much of the old has been purged out. The second generation does not have to surmount the old walls of heathenism. Real Pentecosts are realized after the school has broken down the old barriers and changed the whole mental make-up. We have a Christian literature, breathe a Christian atmosphere, inherit Christian customs, live in the presence of churches, grow up in Christian or semi-Christian homes, and the golden thread of Christian philosophy runs through all we learn and think. It is not so in the non-Christian world. The mind of the cultured pagan is filled with the ideals and practices of his faith, and the social custom that has been fixed upon him by immemorial habit is never questioned. The savage heathen mind is undeveloped; he is the creature of dread superstition; nature is full of demons, and religion is a thing of fear. He has no scientific processes of thinking and is a sublime egoist. His social life is narrowed to the necessities of his selfish career and no man trusts another for good. The children of the mission schools are given a new mind, a new conception of the universe and of the past, and the seeds of a better life philosophy are planted in their thinking. The result is an accessibility to Christian truth on the part of many who do

173

not possess the spiritual enterprise necessary to acquire the faith that comes with a proclamation of the Word. A minority do possess that spiritual enterprise and have hearts so open that the evangel grips them and changes their lives, their instruction following their conversion; but the majority need the soil of their souls tilled and prepared for comprehension of the truth. The school has thus been one of the most fertile of evangelistic agencies. Bishop Tucker, of Uganda, tells of their evangelistic garnering during the five years from 1902 to 1907; they baptized 36,000, or more than 7,000 annually, and so many enrolled as inquirers that it was with difficulty they could give them instruction. In South India to-day, after mature schooling and a generation of successful work, there are so many pressing for entrance into the church that the missionaries are actually not able to give the necessary preliminary examinations as fast as they are requested; single fields have had as high as 3,000 accessions in a year. John Mott conducted an evangelistic campaign among the students of Tokio that brought several hundred into the church, and has recently addressed student meetings in Egypt and among Mohammedans that taxed the capacity of the largest theaters and turned many away. It is safe to say that the faith of the Bishop of Madras, that 50,000,000 low caste men of India are ripe for the gospel, would be wrought into results if there were enough mission schools to reach them all. The rising tide of universal intelligence in India is unloosing them from the bonds that enthralled their minds and led them to accept their portion as one of the dispensations of fate. If they could be led to see that, under Christianity, there is no caste, but an open way to make themselves the real saving salt of India, they would bring a democracy to the nation that would overturn all her traditions and give her a basis for real independence. Every chapel in Korea is also a schoolhouse, and the evangelistic wave that is sweeping that nation is not of the perfervid variety, but based upon a real discipleship, a mind that is instructed in the elements of Christian truth. Dr. Laws, of Livingstonia, says their vital evangelism is in their schools where 16,000 pupils are daily taught Christian living. To leaven the social life of a people is to conduct a very real evangelism, and the reaction upon the life of the church is sure and permanent. "A sound Christian is always a well instructed Christian," says Dr. Hetherwick, of the Blantyre Mission.

CHAPTER V

The Missionary and the Affairs of the World

1. THE MISSIONARY AND OTHER POWERS OF PROGRESS.

"History shows no example of mere civilization elevating a sunken people," says Dr. Warneck. The heroic James Chalmers said he traveled all the South Seas, saw every kind of people, shared bed and board alike of savage and civilized, and that he never saw one place where mere commerce or political interference had by themselves taken positive and permanent good to the child-peoples. The story of the mingling of East and West is a tale of vice and crime, where it has not been relieved by the influences of those men who have not gone for the purposes of selfish gain. Gladstone said, "European intercourse with the uncivilized has, without exception, been disastrous unless attended by missionary exertions." The port cities of the Orient are famous for their wickedness; when two races meet they offer each other the worst they possess. The missionary is the one man who goes without selfish intent, and whose determination is to take social redemption and every other reform that will redound to the good of the people of the land. The trader goes for gain, and the soldier with a mission that compels him to look upon the native as an inferior, fit only for subjection. The missionary seeks to understand the native man and to enter into a sympathetic relationship. He denies himself all the multitudinous opportunities that a new area may offer in way of personal gain, through the use of his expert knowledge of native needs, and devotes himself to an unselfish service. The trader may sell rum, or buy labor, or take advantage of ignorance to charge ten or fifty prices for materials that are really of little worth, but the missionary warns against such nefarious traffic and teaches the victim of it how to supply his own needs. Chulalangkorn, the late progressive king of Siam, said, "The American missionaries have done more to advance the welfare of my country than any other foreign influence." "The missionaries are doing more for the civilizing and educating of the masses of the East than any other agency whatsoever," said a British M. P.

The missionary can not be a political emissary. He does not interfere in matters of government, but he can intercede. His intercession has been denominated interference by those who found their selfish designs frustrated, and it is to such as them most of the charges against missionaries can be traced. In savage lands he is regularly called upon to intercede for the poor victims of savage injustice. He rescues slaves, saves women from cruelty, children from desertion, arbitrates in personal disputes, and advises those who plead for a better order of things. He goes to soften asperities, mould hearts to a love of community peace, found ideas of democracy, and give new well springs of action. Through these things he exerts a vast, indirect influence upon government and society. He rarely joins the revolutionaries, but the lessons he teaches compel progress, and there are times when the masses must suffer death or fight for their right to live in peace with their new ideals; such times are rare, and the arts of peacefulness the missionary uses usually prevent any outbreaks of violence over his revolutionary principles. In Korea all missionary influence was against armed resistance to Japanese occupation; it would have been suicidal, and the experienced missioners thought the better way was to submit to the inevitable and move for the best possible terms in equity and native right to a part in public affairs. This was not done on behalf of imperialism, but on behalf of peace, the saving of life, and a more secure freedom in the future.

In implanting ideas of democracy and personal right the missionary roots into the hearts of men influences that make it impossible for them to submit supinely to oppression and injustice. The leaven of ideas ferments the lump, and men come into their own. The Christian community becomes a sort of Puritan nucleus in the old society; it stands for justice and righteousness, and human nature responds to the call for more benign rulership, once the possibility of its realization is shown. In a savage tribe any progressive is liable to be fixed upon by the witch doctor as a danger to his dread power, and made to suffer for any innovations; if in a more cultivated, though static civilization, he is feared as an innovator who threatens revered customs, and does violence to the memory of the fathers and sages, and is quickly suppressed or violently put out of the way. The late Empress Dowager, before she accepted the inevitable through the failure of the Boxer rebellion, had sundry editors executed by slicing them up a few inches at a time, because they dared turn reformer, and the young emperor is known to have been a royal prisoner until the day of his death.

The cultivating of ideals of democracy and personal right lift a people into self-assertive integrity, and they evolve for themselves a better order of political and social life. Efforts to force upon them things that may be for their benefit, but for which they are not prepared, and which they do not understand, are liable to be disastrous. This is the danger of colonial rule. Superstitions, traditions, and ancient customs are deeply grounded into their nature, and it is more than the task of a day to uproot them without destroying the community life. Poor bonds as they may be, they are nevertheless the bonds that give a social control, and with all their evils society will disintegrate if they are crushed without substituting better.

It has been charged that the missionary, by taking white contact, takes ultimate death to the primitive peoples, that clothing and industry are their enemies, and that changed habits unfit them for their environment. Where the missionary has been left to create his new order without the interference of other whites, there has been a steady increase in population. Such isolated islands in the South Seas show from one to three per cent increase in numbers annually. The

179

charge that the Hawaiians are dying out is refuted by missionaries who have lately made a thorough investigation of the subject; they are not only increasing in numbers, but in wealth, and in their interest in Christianity. Where governmental interference has modified the efforts of the missionary to create a self-supporting people of initiative and industry, by making them recipients of lands they did not need, and of pensions they did not earn, encouraging them thus to live in idleness, they have not kept pace with civilization; most of the American Indians and many of the Maoris of New Zealand are examples of this, though there are many individuals who have arisen to places of influence; Maoris sit in the legislature of New Zealand, and there are instances of American Indians arising to prominence in scholarship and statesmanship. Even where the white race has brought its wholesale influence for good and bad, and contributed so largely of the latter, because the ignorance and childlike character of primitive peoples afford little resistance to the barterers of vice, there are virile qualities of racial character that withstand the contact. There are races in South Africa that have increased population from double to quadruple former numbers in a single generation. It is another pledge of missionary efficiency to learn that these peoples are those which he reached before the trader's caravan came, and that his ideals of temperance and personal integrity had taken hold. Civilization goes by war, politics, trade, or missions. Missions do not claim to be the only civilizing influence, but they do claim to be the most fundamental and unselfish. The missionary is the

Hospital Ward in Kiukiang, Central China. Its contrast to the old native quackery tells marvelously the story of missionary science and benevolence.

only white man who goes for the first time to a barbarous or other alien race for the express purpose of being their friends, and he is the only one of the above envoys that carries with him a confidence that every race can be elevated to a plane of self-sufficiency, and that the benign influence of personal service is the greatest force for the task. All the others, historically, have made subject peoples, and exploited them for gain; the missionary alone vicariously bears their burdens and has faith that they will become sufficient unto themselves by instruction and experience. He does not deny the power of politics and trade, he welcomes them, but he would not deliver any people over to any influence that would make mart of them, or fail to bring good tidings of peace. His implanting of the fundamental principles of manhood and social good carry his influence into all those more remote, though inevitable movements of government, law, commerce, and material advancement that follow an awakened consciousness and are used in the making of an era of progress.

2. THE POLITICAL INFLUENCE OF THE MISSIONARY.

The missionary creates a new type of citizenship. Like Paul of old, he is loyal to the powers that be and renders Caesar his dues, but his great purpose is that God shall have his portion. His work is the creation of a sense of personal freedom and of social responsibility, and the putting of a good conscience into all men. Non-Christian governments are generally arbitrary; there is little sense of citizenship; rule is from above, and governments do not derive just powers from the consent of the governed. All arbitrary rulership partakes of the tyrannical, and, though democracy has its corruptions, oligarchies are notoriously for the benefit of the few. Buckle says no man ever received great arbitrary powers without abusing them. In China all centers in the emperor, who is "The Son of Heaven," and theoretically, the father of his people; each province has a viceroy, who is, if a strong character, all but supreme in his state; under him are a series of officials, each with absolute powers in his realm, and accountable only to the man next above him; there are nine grades of these officials, reaching from the emperor down to the local magistrate. The local magistrate is a petty despot over the populace; to them he is virtually king, and his authority is supreme, save as exceptional appeal may be made over his head. The Chinese were taught a certain peculiar sense of democracy by Confucius, and appeal and rebellion are the final resorts. This absolute officiary is notoriously corrupt. As one of them told a traveler, "We are all worthy of execution, but if the emperor took off our heads, the next set would be as bad." The fault is in the sense of citizenship. In the mission churches the membership learns the rudiments of self-government and acquires a democracy of spirit that makes them prize it. The Viceroy, Tuan Fang, declared that "the awakening of China may be traced in no small measure to the hand of the missionary." He planted the seeds of the new order, and in his education of youth gave a sense of freedom of personality, and of responsibility for the universal welfare, that creates a genuine patriotism. Arthur Smith says the Chinese had no real sense of patriotism in former days; all officials were looked upon as public parasites and a necessary evil; the spirit of the people was that every man must look out for himself at any odds, and as a result government was not a public concern so much as a necessity that had to be endured, and in which each would do well to make the best of it for personal benefit. To-day the new patriotism has taken hold of the educated young men with the power of a religious zeal. It was given inception and has been cultivated in all mission schools, and every influence that the missionary could bring to bear has been in its favor. It is not confined to port cities and places where China has come into contact with material civilization; the west of China is furnishing many of the most progressive men, and is believed by residents in that section to be responding even more rapidly than any other to the call of the new era. "The missionaries," says Tuan Fang, "have borne the light of civilization into every nook and corner of the empire." Dr. Yen, Secretary of the Chinese Legation at Washington, gives "a large part of the credit for instituting this wonderful educational movement to missionary enterprise and foresight." Of missionary influence in Japan, Prince Ito said, "Japan's progress and development are largely due to the influence of missionaries, exerted in the right direction when Japan was first studying the outer world." The work of Guido Verbeck has already been noted. The fact that the emperor conferred signal honors upon him and that the government buried him with all the tokens of national respect, testify eloquently to his part in its remaking. He has been called "The Father of the Japanese Constitution."

The missionary exerts a direct influence upon rulers in many cases. The makers of the new Japan made Verbeck's home their refuge for councils. Dr. Underwood's parlor, in Korea, was the scene of many conferences of the foremost men of the kingdom in the days of transition. Both these men, and many others, thus became privy councilors of the reform party, and to their credit always used their positions to exert an influence that would make for peaceful revolution; they were teachers, not political leaders. When Verbeck was allowed to do nothing more than teach English, he used the New Testament and the Constitution of the United States for his text-books; the lessons were not lost. The Christian literature societies have sowed the seed of all progressive ideas of enlightenment through their translation and distribution of books, and counted that by such indirect methods they were doing real missionary work through doing good to humanity, bringing the revolutionary forces of new ideas into the minds of the leaders of a nation. The late Emperor of China was made a reformer through books supplied by the Society for the Diffusion of Christian Knowledge, and his chief adviser, the great reformer and exile, Kang Yu-Wei, said, "I owe my conversion to reform and my knowledge of reform to the writings of two great missionaries, Dr. Timothy Richard and Dr. Allen."

In barbarous lands the influence of the missionary is as much more direct as the need is greater and the enlightenment of the ruler less. "Savages are made into law-abiding citizens by missionaries better than by any other process," said the Governor of New Guinea. A British Commodore in the waters of that same savage island said, "These gentlemen have established such a hold over the natives as many a crowned head would be glad to possess." Once the missioner gains their confidence, he becomes an all-powerful influence in their tribal life. He is called upon to settle disputes between tribes, and wards off many a bloody battle. The history of heroic, personal interventions on behalf of peace would fill an inspiring volume. Savage justice scarcely deserves the name; it is fraught with arbitrary judgment, if not with trial by some process of superstition instead of upon the merits of the case, and the accused is regarded as guilty until some fate established his innocence. The missionary intercedes for justice and teaches the arts of its administration to the chieftains. In the South Seas they wrote whole codes, notably in Tahiti and Raiatea, and saw them adopted by the voice of chieftains, and approved of the people. Ex-Secretary John Foster said that the political reorganization of those islands was almost entirely the work of missionaries. Whole communities were persuaded to move from low to high lands for the sake of health, were reorganized in government, given a better type of architecture and agriculture, and persuaded to write permanent pacts of peace with ancient enemies. In Africa the missionary has to his credit several reformed governments among savage tribes, any one of which would be well worth the whole missionary exertion in that continent. Khama the Good is one of the notable names of native African history. His government of the Bechuannas has been a model in primitive control. He abolished slavery, polygamy, and concubinage, established industry, absolutely prohibited intoxicants, and set up courts that substituted justice by fair trial in place of the old barbarities of trial by ordeal and the whims of the witch doctor. There has been no war under his administration, whereas before war was the chief business of the people; the traveler has been made safe anywhere in his realm, and trade is carried on with even more sense of right on behalf of the black man than on behalf of the white man, who all too often comes prepossessed with the idea that he is a superior being, and that it is "no harm to cheat a nigger." The story of Coillard's influence over Lewanika is but little less thrilling than that of Moffat's over Africaner; from a bloody and drunken despot he was converted into a sober, just ruler, and though not professing Christianity openly, as Khama and Daudi have done, he lives well up to its ethical code and has transformed his country. The transformation of Uganda has been spoken of heretofore. The influence of the missionaries has reached on out to the west of Uganda and made quite as notable conquests. Daudi, king of Toro, is one of the most remarkable of African chieftains. He has led his people into new ways of peace, and preaches Christianity both to them and to neighboring tribes. He has gone to those with whom he was perpetually at war, and, in the name of the new peace, exhorted them to accept his way of life and government. Many such narratives could be given

186

of South Sea chieftains. Thokambau, of Figi, was one of the most notable in missionary annals. He was a man of exceptional forcefulness and had used his power up to the limits of savage brutality. The list of his victories and of the horrible feasts he had provided from bands of prisoners taken was long. He lived for a quarter of a century as a Christian ruler, and saw the new order established over a citizenship that could read and write, and that worshiped the God of peace in peace. Often he looked upon the orphaned and the widowed whose sad fate was of his making in the days of his savagery, and wept in pleas for forgiveness. It is the glory of the missioner that he was able, in most cases, to bring about the change without bloodshed, though there have been times when the party of re-action and savagery, because they were the beneficiaries of the inequalities and cruelties of the old system, have made war upon the party of peace and progress. In such times the cause of right had to be defended, but victory was ever celebrated with forgiveness and an effort to win the vanquished to the better way.

Loyalty and a better type of citizenship is ever the missionary's aim. When the powers were threatening to partition China, the missionaries were fast friends of the empire and gave all influence to its maintenance. During the war with Russia the missionary body passed strong resolutions of loyalty to Japan. They were among the first to advocate repeal of "extra territoriality." In India they have ever plead the cause of the people, if not according to the ideals of the more radical political elements, at least on behalf of justice to the native and a humane administration of law.

187

British administrators give them credit for suggesting many emendations of law that were for the popular good, made possible through their thorough and sympathetic understanding of the common life. In Korea they exerted all influence in favor of a purer government, and native Christians refused to submit to the demands of corrupt officials, though they scrupulously obeyed the law and paid the legal tax. Their action was strong in calling attention to official corruption, and when the revolution began it was held on its course through the influence of a club that was predominantly Christian, loyal to the king, and persistent in its demands for reform at his hands.

The missionary is not a political emissary, but the welfare of a people is so intimately bound up with its political destiny, that in influencing them for a better manhood and more humane ways of life he must indirectly, at least, influence their political destiny. That influence is positive for a larger participation of the common people in government, and, through the popular education given in mission schools, there is raised up a generation of men who are able both to obtain it and maintain it. The missionary does not go to create republics, but he does go to create a citizenship, and whether the form of government be republican or monarchical, it must be more democratic as the masses rise in intelligence and personal responsibility, and the change will always be ushered in by the arts of peaceful revolution if the influence of the missioner is dominant in the councils of reform.

3. MAKING TWO BLADES OF GRASS GROW WHERE ONE GREW BEFORE.

Booker T. Washington said that if he had to choose between sending his graduates to Africa to preach salvation in another world, or to teach the natives how to make two blades of grass grow where one grew before, he would choose the latter. He believes that it does little good to preach an otherworldliness and leave men in the old sordid environment of this present world. Fortunately there is no such alternative. We no longer hear the plea that we must hasten to the heathen because so many millions are plunging annually into an eternal abyss of fire. Not more than twenty years ago some of our greatest boards made belief in that sort of doctrine an essential in a missionary candidate. To-day we go, as Dr. Clark puts it in his little volume on "A Study of Christian Missions," to "plant" rather than to "rescue." Jesus did not come merely to save a few out of the world, but to save the world. So the missionary goes to save individuals and through them to save a world, and he has faith that the little band of "Jesus men," as they are generally called, will be the saving salt of society. Everywhere he makes two blades of grass grow where one grew before, and, increasing the capacity of men to appreciate and use the material factors of civilization, he builds up a self-supporting society of more advanced grade, and creates an environment that makes it possible for them to enjoy the benefits of progress.

The missionary creates new wants. Without the desire for things not yet possessed, the more primitive

189

and backward civilizations could not be lifted beyond their present attainments. The primitive man is not a creature of many wants; he is satisfied with provision for immediate needs, therefore he is not industrious. The chase and warfare seem to him more direct means of satisfying his desires, so he resorts to those sporadic and cruel arts and despises the cultivation of nature as the work of those who can not fight and hunt. This indignity done, the art of labor condemns woman-kind to the status of a slave, military necessity creates despotism, and the tribe is condemned to penury or starvation, if it be not successful in its barbarous enterprises. The missionary changes the ideals of economy and substitutes honest toil for rapine, teaching the native that it is easier, and much more sure, for him to cultivate nature and become the recipient of her lavish gifts than it is to prey upon man and wild beast, and put his livelihood under a gamble of luck, or at the stake of battle.

Among primitive peoples especially this lays upon the missionary the necessity of training whole popula-tions in the arts of industry. The work of industrial schools has been treated in a former chapter. The industrial work of the missionary is not confined to that of the industrial school; it is limited only to the industrial needs of the Christian community he founds. The poverty-stricken methods of industrial economy must all be revised and the implements of more pro-gressive ways introduced. We have already seen how thousands of plows were introduced into the fields of East Africa by the Livingstonia, Blantyre, and Zam-besi missions. The same thing was done in India, and small American plows replaced the ancient pointed stick by tens of thousands. The missionary adapted looms and cotton gins to native necessities in India, and introduced them into Africa together with the cultivation of cotton. The Scotch mission on Lake Nyassa started coffee growing, and wheat was introduced into Uganda, New Zealand, and in many other fields. In India a superior method of milling the grain was taught and the machinery necessary brought from abroad by missionary hands. In China many missionaries have become especially interested in problems of agriculture, and have given to the hard-working and economical Chinese farmer methods of intensive cultivation that have made work much more productive and life by that much less hard. In semi-arid lands he has taught the arts of irrigation, and in China improved the wells and canals that had been used from time immemorial for the watering of the fields. In Assam tea culture was begun, and orange growing was taken to the South Seas. A partial list of the edibles introduced in various lands will give some idea of the scope of his industrial activities in the task of giving peoples a better chance in life. He has transplanted oranges, limes, mangoes, cocoanut palms, cocoa beans, pine-apples, coffee, cotton, tomatoes, wheat, barley, corn, and almost every other edible adaptable to the land in which he happened to find the necessity; he has transported cattle, builded boats, laid out roadways, constructed houses, moulded brick, dug canals, cultivated fields, established mercantile houses, and contributed every art of material progress as an aid to his beneficent work of creating a civilization. The Zulu mud hut became a neat, square cottage, with tile roof; the Syrian hovel became a two-storied house with chimneys where before the smoke had escaped through a hole in the thatch, and with tiled floor, where before there was only a hole in the mud wall; the South Sea common shed, where from forty to sixty persons of all ages and both sexes lived in common, was changed into separate family houses; Hindu villages have been so changed that travelers can always tell they have felt the impress of Christianity. Peoples who roved from place to place, following the luck of the chase, have been induced to settle into stable communities and till the ground for a living, substituting substantial dwelling-places for the bed of sand and the shelter of bower or cave; the sheet iron stove has been substituted for the charcoal brazier or the brick oven in which weeds and grass were burned and warmth given the limbs of little children that had suffered severely with the only slightly tempered cold of closed and stifled rooms.

The missionary has developed native products and created new types of native implements and put peoples on their own resources. In the South Seas he discovered the uses of arrow-root and taught the native how to make it one of the staples of life. He dug wells and showed the wondering savages how to quench their thirst when there was no rain, and moved plantations back from the miasmatic lowlands of stream beds to the healthier uplands. He has induced communities to remove their villages from sandy and arid lands to richer soil by adapting novel products to their native arts of cultivation. It is claimed he invented the jinrikisha, and thus gave Japan its chief vehicle. The Khaki dye is one of his African discoveries, and many medical remedies can be traced to his study of botany. He produced a movable type for Japanese character and invented typewriters for the Burmese and Chinese, the latter with four thousand characters on its type wheel. John Williams taught the South Sea Islanders how to build ships, and they became quite adept, substituting vessels of several hundred tons burden for their old "dugouts." In East Africa Mackay built some two or three hundred miles of roadway and thus began the innovation that has replaced miles of winding native paths with excellent roadbeds. The Lake Nyassa mission builded the famous Stevenson road joining Lakes Nyassa and Tanganika. Everywhere his effort has been so to create the arts of industry, the desire for a better manner of living, and so to develop native resourcefulness that every community would become self-sufficient, able to provide for its own higher wants, or so to contribute to those of other places that trade would bring all the means for a better manner of life, and thus allow the stable attainment of those higher intellectual and spiritual states which are conceived to be the goal of life.

As the material adjuncts of better living depend upon the creation of new desires, so their use and maintenance depend upon the building up of a sense of honesty, of community service, the practice of the golden rule in business and industrial relationships, and the necessity of economy and self-dependence. The common people of India, like our negro masses in the South, live on credit. They are forever in debt, and the usurer is pitiless; the lowest rate of interest is one per cent per month, the average annual rate is from 20% to 30%, and often runs as high as 70%. In China and Moslem lands the rate will run from one to three per cent per month, and in Siam it runs up to 100%. There is literally no limit upon the power or avariciousness of the native money lender, and he enforces his legal rights with Shylock severity. The debtor's prison is a crushing institution, and slavery is the nemesis of the hopeless debtor. The missionary cultivates a thrift that escapes the usurer, and, where necessary, founds savings institutions, co-operates with the government in inducing the people to use Agricultural Banks, or adopts the English Provident Societies as means for defeating the all-consuming dragon of interest. Retail trade is a process of haggling over prices and rests upon the theory that one must get, not what an article is worth, but what another may be induced to pay for it. The missioner lends all influence to more open and scientific methods of commerce, and to the cultivation of that trust of one another that makes trade one of the constructive arts of a civilized life, instead of a barbarous method of taking advantage of necessity. In numerous instances the native Christian has built up a renumerative business by practicing the simple arts of open dealing, making every article just what he represented it to be, with the price plainly marked upon it. By elevating the moral standards he cultivates a character that is able to appreciate the benefits of a more progressive material civilization, and by

Reid Christian College, Lucknow, India, illustrating the most attractive type of native architecture—used in educating a progressive generation.

introducing the arts of a more progressive material civilization he fortifies the moral and social life he has planted with an environment that sustains and upbuilds it.

4. THE PIONEER OF CIVILIZATION.

The missionary is the pioneer of civilization. He discovers new realms, explores unknown regions, opens trade routes, establishes friendly relations with barbarous and hermit peoples, and cultivates a universal desire for the arts and goods of civilization. The Chinese Ambassador to the United States calls him "the frontiersman of trade and commerce." The emissaries of world trade have gone to the Orient prejudiced against him, and returned to proclaim him "the advance agent of business," and the greatest benefactor of the Orient. A certain commercial man went to China with all the prejudice a materialistic mind and an ignorance of missions could create; in Shanghai he drank a toast to commerce and proclaimed aversion to the missionary; six months later he returned to the same club to praise the emissary of Christianity as the choicest product of modern civilization, the harbinger of all progress, and the greatest asset that commerce possessed in the Orient. He is not a "drummer," nor does he go with any avowed attempt to open trade routes, or act as an advance agent for Western commerce. But so surely as he elevates a people he creates within them the desire for things that civilized industry alone can produce, and by piercing new lands and exploring unseen regions he opens avenues for the trader. He has little interest

195

in trade as such; in fact he often finds the frontier trader his chief enemy, for he deals in rum, firearms, opiates, and much useless material, and generally takes sinful advantage of the guilelessness of the primitive man. True exchange of commodities is one of the promoters of civilization, and between it and the missionary cause there is a large community of interest, but the brutal trade in men, known as the "Kanaka traffic" in the South Pacific Seas, the "red rubber" commerce of the Congo with its unspeakable oppression and brutality, the opium trade in China with its resultant "Opium War," the merchandise of cocoa and its accompanying slavery in Portuguese West Africa, and the universal decimation from rum wherever it has been taken, constitute a series of evils for which civilized powers can make no apology. The missionary has heroically protested against all these evils. John G. Paton labored arduously to obtain the international agreement protecting primitive peoples against the expert of rum and firearms from civilized lands. The missionary body in China have always protested vigorously against the enforced opium trade. Two missionaries, Drs. Morrison and Shepherd, at risk to their work and their lives, and by submitting to arrest and harassment, were influential in bringing about a change in the governmental supervision of the Congo regions that promises to abolish the oppressive system of taxation and the cruelties of "red rubber." The missionary protest against the "Kanaka traffic" in the South Seas brought stringent laws against it, and finally abolished the whole system of indenture upon which it hung. Wherever white men have traded

196

in the flesh of the blacks, the Protestant missionary has been at enmity with him. The work of Livingstone in abolishing the slave trade in Africa needs no rehearsing here. He declared he went to open roads for commerce and missions, and to substitute trade in commodities for the universal African trade in men. The result was that African Companies were formed. British naval vessels patrolled the African coasts in quest of Arab slave dhows, and new forms of currency were introduced in place of the old standard of exchange, which was expressed in the value of a slave.

Civilization brings new wants, and new wants mean exports. Dr. Dennis says a careful estimate made by Englishmen, the greatest of all world traders, was that every pound spent on missions brought back ten pounds in commerce, and quotes another authority as saying that "when a missionary has been on the field twenty years he is worth $50,000 per year to British commerce." A study of African communities showed that after they were Christianized they used ten times as much merchandise as before. To teach a million people to wear clothes means an immense trade in cotton, and to persuade them to keep their clothes and faces clean brings demands for soap. When missionaries first went to Syria there was not a window glass in the country. They introduced both window glass and stoves, and nearly every house in Asia Minor is now supplied. The trade in plows in Africa and India has already been noted. The statistics Dr. Dennis gives of trade in the South Seas totals millions annually, and is directly traceable to missionary labors. That of the Lake regions of Africa is no less due to missionary pioneering and the transformations wrought in the desires of a barbarous population. Wu Ting Fang wittily remarked that if we could induce Chinamen to lengthen their shirt-tails one inch it would make the cotton-growers of the South rich. The missionaries to China have opened museums, illustrating the material and other achievements of civilization, and as many as 100,000 have passed through their doors in one year's time. They have established "model stores" to introduce those implements of progress that would be of profit to their communities and conducted them, without an eye to profit, until normal channels of trade could be opened. Many mission schools have business departments for the training of the youth in the ways of upright commerce, and every school gives instruction in the things of universal interest, the life and work of the world, and the advantage of open communication with all mankind.

The missionary has not laid down railroads, but his work has expedited their construction. The first successful train traffic in North China was conducted along a route where there had been a line of mission stations for twenty years; other roads were angrily torn up by the coolies and their friends, who saw a single locomotive doing the work of hundreds of men. The missions had so made for progress that the people were ready for the innovations it brought. To-day there are 6,000 miles of railroad in China and as much more projected; the Chinese will probably be the greatest railroad builders of the century. Africa will ere long be traversed both from east to west and

198

from north to south by direct lines of rail and steamboat traffic. It was the missionary, Krapf, who first designed an eastern to western route by means of a transcontinental line of mission stations, and Bishop Gray dreamed long before Cecil Rhodes of a Cape to Cairo route by means of a continuous line of mission stations and traversible roadways connecting them. It was Mackay who first suggested the Uganda railroad. Wherever the missionary goes the trading-ship, the railroad, and the telegraph follow in course of time. He is not the sole creator of trade routes, and in some instances the trader has preceded him, but the rule has been that he pioneered the way, and it has ever been that he first found that way into the hearts of the people which Stanley called the greatest achievement.

Where there has been no open means of trade, or no honest means at hand, the missionary has founded trading companies as adjuncts to his work of creating a civilization. He has never conducted the commerce himself for the advantages of profit; if it was necessary to establish a commerce he did it as a means to his one task of converting men to Christianity and building a civilized community in which they could retain their new-found life, and he relinquished it upon the first opportunity that offered. The Uganda Company, the Scottish Missions Industries Company of the Blantyre Mission, the Livingstonia Trading Company of the Livingstonia Mission, the Papuan Industries of New Guinea, and the Basle Mission Trading Company are instances of commercial auxiliaries formed by missionary men, independent of missionary societies, and for the specific purposes of working in harmony with missionary activities. Their purpose is to give the natives a social environment in which they can develop Christian character, to enable them to become independent, to make the mission self-supporting, and to protect them against unscrupulous traders. These companies superintend plantations, develop the cultivation of sugar, cotton, coffee, and rubber, make bricks, build houses, transport goods, build lake vessels, construct roads, and give all possible financial and instructional encouragement to natives in the building up of independent farms and businesses of their own. They are typical examples of philanthropy and five per cent, with great emphasis upon the philanthropic part of enterprise. They furnish models in business enterprise and examples in business integrity. Josiah Strong advocates a plan to send superior Christian young men to the mission fields as merchants, commercial men, investors, and superintendents of all manner of enterprises conducted there by the whites. He would make them an antidote to those worshipers of mammon and devotees of materialism that go with a spirit of adventure to the conduct of such enterprises, and also a positive force for the introduction of Christian ethics into those commercial relations that so often afford difficulties to the non-Christian mind in its wrestle with the appeal of the missionary.

The missionary is a maker of men and civilization. Among the necessities of his work are the arts of material progress. He needs them to supply the newly awakened wants, and to furnish an environment in which the awakened lives of men can find safety. Sir Hiram Maxim, an advocate of materialism, wrote a virulent attack on the missionary; he used unbecoming language even in the violence of his prejudices against both the man and his method. The Chinese Courts have interdicted its circulation in China, one of the judges on the Supreme Bench at Shanghai saying, "I never read such balderdash." There is no conflict between honest commerce and the missionary, nor between the arts of material progress and his work of awakening the souls of men. Commerce and politics owe him a vast debt for his work of exploration, of creating new wants, of opening closed and savage lands to civilization, and for his transforming and peace-making evangel.

5. THE MISSIONARY AND UNIVERSAL PEACE.

The dominating world movement of our time is that toward universal peace. There has not been a great war between Western nations in the last generation. To-day there are no less than sixty arbitration treaties in force, and such international agreements bid fair to grow rapidly, both in number and in the scope of their provisions. The nations are drawn together with numerous common agreements; the Navigator's Code is used by forty of them alike, and the International Postal and Telegraphic Union includes fifty-five. International conferences include every conceivable question that is of common concern, from a general conference on morals up to the Inter-parliamentary Union and The Hague Tribunal. The Central American Peace Union is an actualized example of enforced conciliation through judicial procedure. The Hague Prize Court bids fair to become the nucleus of a universal court of arbitration. The American Bureau of Republics, including twenty-one nations, is so educating the Americans on the commonality of their enterprises that war will become impossible as public opinion receives education. The Red Cross is an unofficial, but none the less real, international bond. International law is becoming a recognized code that will demand a court, and rules of war have the force of international legislation. The neutralization of territory is one of the most signal signs of a "Truce of God" in our times. The Baltic and North Seas are now neutralized in the interest of common safety, and various ones of the smaller nations are guaranteed against attack by the power of stronger governments; such is the case with Switzerland, Belgium, and Norway.

The growth of common knowledge, the widening sympathy that a more universal education brings, the common interests of an international commerce that is making the whole world one vast trading mart, the rising intelligence of labor and its awakening to the fact that it bears all the burdens in the end, the tendency of all legislation to take on a social cast, and the evolving spirit of humanitarianism, all make mightily against warfare. The ideals of one age work out into action in the next. Kings and diplomats can no longer make war. "The people now, not governments, make friendships or discord, peace or war, between nations," said Secretary Root. It is gratifying to have Secretary Yen, of the Chinese delegation, declare that "There is a public opinion in China now that makes itself heard," for it has been the fear of the West that the Yellow man would arise to avenge the wrongs done him. If it is left to public opinion there will be no "Yellow Peril," for the masses of China are peaceful by nature and through long habit. "They believe, philosophically, in the right so thoroughly," said Sir Robert Hart, "that they scorn to think it requires to be enforced or supported by might."

When we turn to the other side of the question and see the vast preparations constantly being made for war, we wonder if there is any real promise of its cessation. The world is staggering to-day under a vast war debt of $35,000,000,000, and goes on spending no less than $2,000,000,000 annually on preparations for battles they hope will never come. There is yet a "military party" dominant in most of the nations. Russia runs up an annual deficit of $75,000,000, but makes plans for a billion dollar navy. France, Germany, Italy, and even England, are in debt until the interest alone is a great burden upon public revenues, and the wages of the laborer are so low as to forbid him the promise of a competence in old age. Even the United States spends hundreds of millions yearly on her army and navy, though she possesses that "magnificent isolation" which ought to take her out of the suspicions of old-world complications. Her population has increased 85% in the last thirty years, her

wealth 185%, and her expenditures 400%, two-thirds
of it for a military budget. Might we not cry with
Katrina Trask:

"Peace is not peace that sings its battle songs,
And sets its cannons on a hundred hills;

Peace is the great affirmative of God;
It knows no armies, arms or armaments;
For armies, arms, and armaments deal death,
And peace holds conquest in the strength of life;
Its crown immortal is unconquerable.

Cease to build battle-ships and death's grim en-
    ginery;
Cease to pay tribute to the god of war;
And cease—O Pharisees—to pray 'Thy Kingdom
    come,'
While you are voting means to make a hell,
In some vain boasted cause of righteousness."

Commerce and politics have been the fruitful
sources of most modern wars. The accusation that
missions have been the cause of conflict is easily refuted. In China the Boxer rebellion afforded opportunity for much materialistic and misanthropic mis-
judgment of missions. That rebellion involved missions only because they were foreign, not because they
were religious, or because of any direct opposition
to the missionary as an emissary of Christianity, or
an opponent of native faiths. Missions is the one
world movement of our time that stands unalterably

opposed to warfare. One nation might listen to the demands of commerce and compel another to open its ports to trade; political consideration might compel the opening of a land like Tibet; but missions never asked for force to open Tibet or any other closed land, though they might wait, like the lonely Moravian at his outpost in the Himalayas, thirty years for the day to come when he could enter in with his message of human good, or like Peter Rijnhart, who was martyred in attempting to win Tibet's friendship, give his own life in an effort to show a hermit folk that the missionary would bring them good if only they would let him come in.

The missioner has brought peace to vast populations that knew no other manner of contact than that of strife and bloodshed. In the South Seas whole tribes were won from the decimating terrors of inter-tribal strife to a peace that has not been broken in two generations. The Fijians number more than 100,000 souls, and a more peaceful land is unknown; John Hunt found them living by war and cannibalism. The Battaks of Sumatra number 50,000, and are to-day a nation of cruel, superstitious, warlike folk, won to the gentle arts of peace. The Sarawaks were among the most dangerous and thieving of aboriginal peoples; an English traveler says that to-day a traveler may drop his portmanteau anywhere on the pathway, ramble in perfect peace where a few years ago his head would have been taken, and return to find his goods untouched. The Zulus were perhaps the ablest and most competent militarists ever discovered among primitive peoples. They had a regular military, organization with companies and corps, and a military law. Their fighting qualities are the equal of any living race, but they were won to arts of peace by the missionaries before the white trader made inroads upon them. In Uganda, Mackay found Mtesa ruling a well organized primitive state. His army, with its regularly constituted series of chieftains, was anything but a savage horde of undisciplined raiders, and was used to prey upon weaker neighboring tribes in a vast slave trade that counted its victims by the thousands. To-day Winston Churchill says he never traveled in a more law-abiding, peaceful land, and lays his tribute of praise upon the head of the missionary.

Wherever the missionary has gone he has been a force for conciliation between the intruding white and the native peoples. He has stood between the arrogance of the colonial administrator or the pioneer trader and the rights of the native races, and his intimate understanding of the native mind and custom has been a source of information to governors who desired to do the best by their primitive wards. Sir Mackworth Mackenzie, Lieutenant Governor of the Punjab, said the lives and teachings of the missionaries are the most potent influence working there. Our first ministers to China found the missionaries indispensable to their work and testified that without them, with their use of the native tongue and their sympathetic knowledge of the native mind, their work would have been impossible. Without a single exception these ambassadors of the early days became warm defenders of missions, and especially of the missionary, as a force making for peace between the nations. It was S. Wells Williams who wrote the "Toleration Clause" in our treaty with China, which was later put into that of England also. He also brought about the "Most Favored Nation Clause" of our treaty with Japan. Dr. Dennis cites numerous specific instances of such direct influence of the missionary in international relations. Missionaries have accepted consulates and sat on government commissions because of the opportunities offered to prevent friction and cultivate comity. Dr. Allen became our first minister to Korea and was a dominant influence in the peaceable opening of that closed land to civilization and contact with the world. Verbeck sent a Japanese commission around the world and opened their eyes to its marvels, resulting in a quick opening of the land to all the influences of civilization, and a proclamation of absolute toleration. The missionary has ever stood for the essential oneness of races and nations; admitting the vast difference in attainments, he believes in the potentialities of even the least among men, if only they be discriminatingly educated and trained through the long period it must take to raise up a civilization. "All conclusions based upon the assumption that the status of a race at any particular moment is to be wholly or largely explained by the physical characteristics of that race, turns out to be an illusion," says Lord Weardale, President of the Universal Races Congress.

Kipling may sing that "East is East and West is West, and never the twain shall meet," but the missionary, pre-eminently the world's cosmopolite, out of his rich experience and sympathetic understanding of peoples, his scientific study of the psychology of racial minds, his explorations into the sociology of all mankind, and his experiments in the creation of civilization, believes that there is a broad and deep foundation of universal human experience that warrants him in contending for a world order of peace and interracial communion that will adjust all difficulties, assure every people of their own independent opportunity to life, liberty, and the pursuit of happiness, and make all mankind one of kin. Peace is bound up in an attitude of mind more than in any external arrangements that can be made. The missionary cultivates that attitude of mind in his instructions in fraternity, his breaking down of provincialism and sectionalism, his demand for equality of human right, his inculcation of a universal religion of humanity, and his presentation of one Father God to all men. Principal Fairbairn said that to have realized Plato's Republic would have ruined humanity. To realize Christ's Kingdom of God alone will save all humanity to peace and fellowship, and lift up that very class whom Plato deemed it impossible to elevate. Chancellor Kent said, "A general diffusion of the Bible is the most effectual way to civilize and humanize mankind." Its circulation is an evangel of ideals; a knowledge of it founds in the minds of men those ideas that break down suspicion and substitute confidence, forbids one preying upon another and demands service one of another, establishes a universal spirit of democracy, and inspires humanity with brotherly love.

208

CHAPTER VI

The Social Way of Unity

1. THE FIELD AND THE KINGDOM.

It is estimated that there are now 1,700,000,000 souls in the world. Of this number only about 550,-000,000 are even nominally Christian. Thus two-thirds of humanity are yet to be evangelized. If we count those vast Catholic and Greek populations that are yet superstitious and idolatrous adherents to a form of Christianity, such as those of South America and the masses of Russia, and add to them the worshipers in the ancient and degenerate churches, such as those of the Copts, the Armenians, and the Nestorians, the number will be increased by 150,-000,000 more. If we estimate the number of Protestants at a round 200,000,000, there yet remains a like number of Roman and Greek Catholics, among whom the millions dwelling in exclusively Catholic lands have great need of a higher social plane of life, to say nothing of the needs of a correct religious conception of the exclusive place of Christ in our faith, of freedom of conscience, and a conception of the practical oneness of religion and righteousness.

If for the sake of our immediate problem we confine ourselves to those peoples who are non-Christian, we are almost appalled at the vastness of the under-

14   209

taking. Here are 200,000,000 Mohammedans who have scarcely been touched. Their vigor as a missionary force has been overestimated, but they are practically the only missionary religion outside Christianity, and that they are pushing an active propaganda in the Soudan and south into Equatorial Africa. The Senussi of the Soudan have a definite organization for propaganda, and are imbued with all the fanatical intolerance of the old-time Moslem. In India Islam makes progress over the native faiths, largely because it destroys caste and appeals to the millions that are under its thralldom among the lower and out-castes, but India is a free country and Mohammedans are won to Christianity. Turkey is opening to the message and Moslems are among the inquirers. Freedom of the press and of speech can not long prevail without freedom of action following. The process may be slow, but "the mills of God grind slowly." Persia is awakening and Mohammedan children are found in her mission schools. In Africa the creeping frontier line could be successfully turned back by a strong line of mission stations from Uganda to the Congo. Islam is not insuperable, though she presents the greatest need for strategy in the statesmanship of the modern missionary church.

India's 300,000,000 present the greatest social need of any of the older lands. She is the oldest of the great missionary fields and there is within her borders to-day a Christian community, counting those who have openly accepted the Christ and those whose lives are more or less ordered after the tenets of Christianity, though not openly associated with any Christian communion, of 5,000,000 souls. This is a small proportion, but when we compare it with historic parallels it is very encouraging, and if we could measure the leavening influence of the missionary force upon the social and national life of the people, we should be fairly astounded at its success. Sir Augustus Rivers Thompson called the missionaries the "true saviors of the empire," and Sir Andrew Fraser told a convention of commercial men that out of thirty years' experience as a government administrator in India, he was convinced that the missionary had done more for her uplift than all other agencies combined. But India's multitudes are yet under the thralldom of superstition and in bondage to caste. Famine devastates her and a million die in one section while plenty is enjoyed in another, yet there will be little charity. Millions live in squalor and die of plague and preventable diseases because they have no physician. She is a vast and rich land, and science and the spirit of humanity would make her equal to all her problems, but she is blinded by her superstitions and enslaved by her anti-social customs.

China's 350,000,000 are in the dawn of the most stupendous change history will have to record. The great lethargic giant is yawning after two millenniums of sleep, and what he will do when fully conscious of his powers will depend upon the manner in which we deal with him. He is naturally peaceable and a lover of industry. If we touch China with that "enchanter's wand" which Darwin found in missionary benevolence, it may be won to the Kingdom of God through those peaceable works whose fruit is righteousness. Sir

211

Robert Hart warned the encroaching nations that they "thought China moved too slowly." "Some day," said he, "you will think she moves too fast." There the masses labor for from six to ten cents per day and devote hundreds of millions to votive offerings at the altars of their false gods. Corruption has reigned so long in all governmental circles that their efforts at material progress will entail vast burdens upon the toiling masses through the historic methods of "squeeze." They have not that sense of truthfulness without which a vast commercial life can never be builded. Indirection characterizes their intercourse, and lack of accuracy makes the forward way tortuous. "China," said President Angell, once American High Commissioner to Peking, "will never be redeemed until she bows the knee to Christ." It is not necessary to recount the story of her suffering millions, even in times of plenty. Poverty is omnipresent, and epidemic disease is reckoned up to spirit forces. Until she receives that Christianity which one of her scholars described as so wonderfully opening the "eye of the mind," she will not successfully be made anew.

Japan's crowded areas have scarcely been touched by the missionary evangel. Her millions are digging sustenance out of her mountain heights and searching for it in the sea. These masses have scarcely been touched by Christianity. The middle and upper classes have heard the message, and ten have been made better by it for every one who has openly identified himself with it in the churches. Prince Ito was one of the party Verbeck sent around the world that they might see what civilization had to offer. In the days of the Revolution he thought Japan needed our Western science and education and all the arts of our material and intellectual progress, but said that their religion was good enough for them. In his later life he commended Christianity for its ethical code, and said that had it not come to his country its young men would have been plunged into excesses of immorality. Count Okuma counsels the youth of Japan to practice the morals of Christianity, and says that without it the developing nation can not hope to endure, for Christian morality is the sure foundation of progress; the thousands that are taught in his school are instructed in Christian morals. Japan needs a morality that will redeem her youth from loose habits and elevate her women to a place beside her men. The 40,000,000 common people have scarcely been touched by the missionary evangel, and a revived Buddhism offers a new challenge among the more educated.

Africa is yet an unoccupied continent. Vast areas of her inner plateaus are unoccupied, and tens of millions have not yet heard that there is a Christ or a Christian civilization. Millions are yet held in slavery in her interiors and cannibalism is still practiced by many tribes. Woman is a chattel, home is unknown, war is the vocation of millions, suspicion paralyzes social life, and humanity lives on a plane little above that of the beasts about it. In the Soudan are unexplored states as vast as Texas, and lines of travel from 3,000 to 5,000 miles in length have no missionary station. The Dark Continent is scarce touched, though where she has been laid under the missionary conquest she has furnished veritable Pentecosts, and the story of the new way of life that has sprung up over the old unspeakable degradation has been like that of Alladin's lamp.

Space will not permit an account of Tibet, just opened to the Gospel after thirty years of waiting at the Moravian outpost in the Himalayas; of the Steppes of Central Asia, with their millions of nomads who live as the ancients did before the days of Abraham; of Siberia, with its frozen stretches of sparsely inhabited territory, and of the islands of the sea where the vileness of man reaches its lowest degree, but where the story of Fiji and the New Hebrides can be retold a hundred times if only the evangel be sent. Suffice it to say that if the marvelous success of missions in the past fifty years is a challenge to greater undertakings, the vastness of the field yet untouched and the need of extension in the lands already entered constitute a call that is tragical in its tone, but that is never discouraging in the light of missionary history, nor in the promises of the God of Nations. To do the work calls for more than the vision and the consecration of the churches; it calls for efficiency at the task as well, for no amount of enthusiasm will avail if it be not so directed as to bring the greatest results. The call for missionary efficiency is a call to unity. Where one puts a thousand to flight, two will chase their ten thousand. The church dare not present other than a united front to the need and to the opportunity.

THE SOCIAL WAY OF UNITY

2. THE THINGS THAT UNITE, AND THE THINGS THAT
   DIVIDE.

Men rarely differ on their knees, nor in the presence
of a recognized human need. Mercy is not denomina-
tionalized, nor has charity ever been the means of
separating Christian peoples into sects. There is
no record of a division in Christendom being brought
about by the doing of good, unless, mayhap, it was
by some who protested against doing it. The great
unifying incentive is a recognition of the task to be
undertaken. The great unifying spirit is an enthusiasm for humanity. Jesus prayed that his disciples
should always be united, in order that the world might
believe he was sent for its salvation. The force that
unites is taking hold of the church in its rising recognition of the needs of the world and the coming of the
faith that convinces it of Christianity's power to save
all men, regardless of race, clime, color, station, or
previous condition. The spirit that unites is taking
hold of the church in the coming of that social conscience which Prof. Francis Peabody characterizes
as the "greatest discovery of the age." It is the social
call, the call of humanity that unites.

The major divisions within the church arose over
questions of conscience. In the larger number of
cases they came because the church, as constituted,
forced the advocates of some new doctrine out of their
fellowship with the intolerance that characterized the
age. Many of the smaller cleavages have been effected
by mere differences of opinion, or by some sectional
or minor difficulty that took root in a time which em-

215

phasized liberty of opinion to the detriment of efficiency in action. But to-day the great contentions for conscience sake have been won and have become the possession of all the churches. Sectarianism stands today as an arrested development. There are no great essentials that longer divide Protestant Christianity into denominations. It is the hold of tradition, the historic continuities, the prejudices of early training, and questions of form and polity, that keep up the walls of division.

The question of unity is not only one of more love and loyalty to Christ, but one of less fealty to the denomination as well. The plea that various denominations present various phases of truth to fit various types of mind falls down utterly before a candid search of fact. On the mission field the practice of "delimitation of territory" annuls such an apology. If Methodists take one field and Baptists another in the Philippines, is it because men have searched and found that one district presents a type of mind that the one denomination fits and the other does not? It is simply because there is a great need, and in its presence all thought of "types of mind" is lost and the two denominations agree together, that, in the interest of their great common cause, they will not divide communities and compete for souls, but will co-operate for their evangelization. And they each find that the other makes quite as good Christians as itself. Missions are saddled with our home divisions, but are trying to meet the issue on the lines of least resistance.

One of the dramatic moments of the Edinburgh Conferences was when a native Chinese delegate addressed the gathering with a plea for union. He reminded the assembled delegates that whatever our traditional differences meant to us, they meant nothing to them. Bishop Root says we must lead the Chinese churches into union or forfeit our right to leadership. In Japan the mission churches tend to unity as rapidly as they become self-supporting. On no field would the denominational divisions long prevail if the churches were self-supporting, nor will they after self-support is possible. The forms of government and the creedal statements we have taken to them are barriers, but they will not be insuperable, for while we have been using them in our evangelization we have been so dominated by the unifying spirit of Christ in the real fundamental work we have been doing, that the spirit will conquer the letter, and union will win over form.

At the New York Ecumenical Conference in 1900 the missionaries pleaded for unity and the delegates from home for comity only. At the Edinburgh Conference in 1910 missionaries denounced sectarianism as a sin and all pleaded for union in the task. Union is coming by way of the mission field. At home we have a Christian civilization and are satisfied. On the mission field there is a pagan or a savage state of society, and the missionary is confronted by such appalling necessities that he is driven to unite all forces to effect their overthrow. The churches at home are less concerned about co-operation in just the measure that they are less concerned about Christianizing the whole earth. To the missionary, confronted by the appalling evils of heathenism, opinions, traditions, forms of worship, and methods of church government

217

count for little, and the victory over heathenism counts
for everything. Their infant churches are surrounded
by heathen practice and need all the help unity can
give. Here at home we are afflicted with a social
inertia that makes movements away from the old moorings difficult. Out on the frontier the worker thinks
less of what means he shall use than that he shall use
the most effective means that can be devised. They
hold fast to eternal principles, but they are much more
ready to adopt working expedients and become all
things to all men, if by any means they may win some.
They are doing what Dr. J. P. Jones, for twenty-five
years a Congregational missionary in India, pleads
that we all do, *i. e.*, "Place more emphasis on the Kingdom of God." We will then, he adds, "Cease to at-
tach so much importance to forms of church organization," and he might have added, as indeed he does
in other words and in many ways, to opinions and
traditional attachments, and to all else that keeps us
apart.

It is emphasis on the Kingdom of God that is most
needed. On the mission field the conception that
Christianity is to be planted in the life and custom
of the people is well grounded. Once men went with
the idea of merely rescuing whom they could from the
lost masses of heathenism. They believed every pagan
faith to be at enmity with God, and entertained little
hope of rescuing whole civilizations and races to a Christian manner of living. To-day the typical missioner
finds much in the native religions that are voices in the
wilderness, pointing to a better way, and he seeks to
show how Christianity fulfills their inadequate leadings.

218

He discovers hidden lodes of human wealth under the debris of heathenism and seeks to bring it to light by his Christian appeal. He pursues the gospel method of winning men one by one, but looks upon each one as new leaven in the lump of native life about him, and lives in the faith that it will take only a considerable minority of such transformed lives to begin to lift up the whole mass. When the leaven begins to work he has a vast force to aid him in the amending social ideals of the unconverted multitudes. Every art that adds to the comfort of life, every moral compulsion that brings a little more of the saving salt of righteousness, every ideal that adds a new star in the pall of darkness and lightens the pathway to unguided feet, every constraint of mercy that softens the heart of heathen hardness, every newly awakened human sympathy, every newly welded bond of patriotism, every abandoned cruelty in ancient custom, and all else that adds to the joy of living, increases fraternity, cultivates sympathy and confidence in human kind, and makes life better worth living, he counts as a part of that "more abundant life" Jesus came to give to men, and as a contribution to the coming of that Kingdom of God he came to establish in the earth.

Missionaries find no difficulty in co-operating in those things that all the world recognizes as matters of Christian charity and righteousness. In those things does the Kingdom of God consist and for them the church was founded. It is only in the measure that Christendom has become concerned over the means whereby the world shall be saved, more than it has over the saving of the world, that it has neglected

219

"righteousness, peace, and joy in the Holy Spirit," while tithing the mint, anise, and cummin of ologies and polities. Less zeal for an ism and more for the weal of men will unite the church in the course of time. There is no denominationalism in easing pain or curing bodies; why should there be in "binding up the broken-hearted," or in the "cure of souls?" The missions co-operate in medical schools and in education. They operate mission presses in co-operation. They present a united front in appeals to governments, and in pro-tests against their detractors. The Mission to Lepers finds no difficulty in operating through all missions. The Christian Literature Societies of China and India and the Religious Tract Society find all doors open to their contributions to the common cause. Union is easy in doing famine or flood or epidemic relief work. United effort has been exerted against such crying social evils as slavery, foot-binding, infanticide, the treatment of woman, the opium traffic, caste, the liquor trade, the Congo atrocities, and every other form of evil that afflicts or threatens humanity. To build two medical schools where one would give more pro-ficient training, or to put hospitals into competition, would not be thought of on the mission field to-day. Books are translated by union committees and used by all. The missions in Japan, West China, and South India issue year books that treat the field as a unity and emphasize the co-operation existing. The *Chinese Recorder and Missionary Journal*, the *West China Missionary News*, and the *United Church Herald of South India* are union journals, and many others co-operate in publication. All contiguous missions meet for prayer and conference.

There is no division in regard to the great fundamentals of doctrine. All missionary communions hold to the Fatherhood of God, the Lordship of Christ, the sufficiency of the Scriptures as a rule of faith and practice, and to the church as representing the living body of the Savior. Each believes that the others are Christian and that they are helping to bring the Kingdom of God into the earth—why should they not labor together to bring it more quickly?

3. BREAKING DOWN THE WALLS OF DIVISION.

The divisions of Protestantism are not ancient, nor are they final. No one denomination expects to absorb all others and become the final church. All recognize that the needs of the world are not met by the things that divide, but by the things that unite. But union will not be the thing of a day, nor will it ever be effected by resolution. Neither will it come through ecclesiastical agreement, but it will come through the gradual drawing together of the churches by the inspiration of an overpowering common objective, and by actual co-operation in the common tasks.

The overwhelming present need is the drawing together of the workers in the common task. It is through unity and co-operation that union will come. The tendencies are shown in great inter-missionary conferences like the Decennial Conference in India, the fourth of which is about to be held; the South

African Conference, three of which have already been held; the Shanghai Conference, which was the first of a series that will become a regular feature of the work in China; the regular Japanese meetings for all missions, and the great Pan-Islamic Conference; all these are cultivating the way to larger co-operation. Sectional conferences are held in almost every field where there are contiguous stations. City associations are uniformly organized in all the mission centers. Departmental meetings to consider various phases of the work cross denominational lines; they are held to consider such problems as education, medical work, literary output, work for women, and industrial training. Such conferences make the workers acquainted and emphasize to their minds the advantages in co-operation and the power in common effort.

In India, West China, and South Africa, Boards of Arbitration have been established. They decide all matters of difference and help to formulate concrete ways and means for co-operation. In the first of these thirty missions are united, every mission board but two accepting the co-operation. In the second every mission and board operating in the territory have joined, and in the last all but one. In the Philippines all but the Episcopalians have entered the "Iglesia Evangelica," or Evangelical Church, and the field is divided so as to prevent overlapping. In Japan all but the high church Anglicans and the American Episcopalians are in the union for promotion of "The Christian Movement in Japan." In Korea the Methodist and Presbyterian bodies have divided the field, and in making the readjustment transferred

Sectional View of Nankin University. This is a union institution, supported by Disciples of Christ, Methodist Episcopal, and Presbyterian Boards.

churches and members from one communion to the other, and that without friction. Indeed, it seemed to add vigor to their common cause. In West China free interchange of members is practiced. India is working to the same end and many missions practice it independently. The mission church can not deny fellowship to one who bears the name of Christ and who is almost sure to be lost amid the overpowering influences of the old heathen life if he is out of fellowship with his brethren; fellowship is given even if full membership is not.

In facing Western civilization China recognizes that the school offers the royal road to progress, and she is founding a national school system. The missionaries are confronted with the task of injecting Christian morals into the new learning of the empire. They find it necessary and easy to rise above denominational lines in giving instruction. Equipment and an able teaching force can not be provided otherwise. Efficiency counts for everything in creating the new education for that empire, for they have long had scholarship and have keen minds for learning. The Nankin University is a union of Methodist, Disciple, and Presbyterian schools. In West China the new university at Chengtu is being founded by the co-operation of all the great missionary societies working there, and the charter provides that all newcomers may have a part in its management upon entering the field. In North China the British Congregationalists and the Presbyterians have a joint Education Association that manages four colleges, supported by these two bodies. In Korea the colleges are union institutions. In India Madras College, one of the famous old Christian schools, has followed the example of the older denominational institutions in the United States by becoming independent and interdenominational. The famous Doshisha in Japan is practically the same. In Shangtung, China, English Baptists, American Presbyterians, and Anglicans co-operate in the management of three colleges, and will unite them into a university after the English plan. All over China the movement for the standardization of all mission schools is progressing, and secretaries to superintend it will be supported jointly. The tendency is strong there for union colleges with Biblical seminaries grouped about them. Yale College at Hankow, Christian College at Canton, and the university projected by Oxford and Cambridge at Hankow, are examples of the effort being made for the education of China by Christian influences that are broader than denominational interests. There are union theological schools at Tokio, Bangalore, Nanking, and Amoy. In Manila a union university is being projected. In Central China a movement is on looking toward the founding of a great union training school for evangelists and native teachers. The leaders of the future church in the mission field will not defend sectarian differences after being educated in the same schools and by the united effort of several denominational boards. In the field of medical training there is little division of effort. In Peking five great societies support one superb school. A like project is under way at Chengtu, in connection with the new union university there, and Nanking University is seeking to found another. Hospitals are supported by denominational societies, but they know no denominational lines in their work; at Iloilo Presbyterians and Baptists have united in the support of one. All medical associations are union, as are all educational associations. There is no division in the doing of good. Union evangelistic efforts are found feasible, and every co-operative effort brings to light new and mightier means for evangelizing the world.

It is very natural for union sentiment to bring about the amalgamation of subdivisions in the larger denominational bodies. This is taking place to a remarkable degree on the mission fields. The best known instance is that of the Presbyterian and Reformed bodies in Japan. Six different synodical bodies have united there and taken the name, "Church of Christ in Japan." The eight Presbyterian bodies in China have divided the empire into six districts, or synods, and are moving toward a national Presbyterian church. It is to be hoped they will adopt the same unifying name they are using in Japan. In India seven churches with the Presbyterial, or representative, form of government have united into The Presbyterian Church in India, while the four working in Korea have formed an independent Presbyterian Church for that Kingdom. The synodical form of government seems to make union easy, because of its representative character. The Episcopal form lends itself less easily to such amalgamation, as each bishopric has a fealty to preserve. In Japan they have a working union that promises a national church with Episcopal government. The Methodists have already united

15   225

there and have a native bishop. As is usual, the native churches found means for union easy; the churches that were supporting them from the home field found assent more difficult. The various Lutheran bodies in all Asiatic fields are moving toward union. In India the various Baptists bodies are uniting. In Madagascar the Congregationalists and other independents found no difficulty in getting together, and likewise in Amoy, China. The more democratic churches of Congregational government have done less in a formal way, but practice a degree of unity that no other missions do, just because there are fewer formalities in the way. Their conferences answer informally where more highly governed ecclesiastical bodies must have formal agreements.

But the union of denominational families is not final. It is a step forward, but the main lines of division are still preserved. Geographical union, or the union of all bodies within a certain territory, is union indeed. This crosses all lines of division and considers only the common good. The Shanghai Conference resulted in the "Christian Federation of China," whose purpose is "to encourage the sentiment and practice of union," and "to hasten the establishment of the Kingdom of God in China." They appointed a committee to stimulate every kind of co-operation and union effort. In Japan the older Evangelical Alliance is undertaking the same kind of effort. At Nairobe, in East Africa, eight missions, representing bodies as far apart as Baptists and Episcopalians, have formed a like working alliance. In West China, one of the virgin fields and a leader in all such forward movements, an Advisory Council has been effective for ten years, and has now issued a declaration favoring "one Protestant Christian Church for West China." They practice free interchange of members just as the churches of one communion do, and all are happy in the fraternal concord of it. In India, after nearly every mission body had passed resolutions favoring it, the great Interdenominational Conference, held at Jubbulpore in 1909, organized "The Federation of Christian Churches in India." They welcome to membership "all churches and societies that believe in God through Jesus Christ, and that accept the word of God as contained in the Old and New Testaments as the supreme rule of faith and practice." They appointed provincial councils and committees on unity, and directed them to secure actual union wherever possible. They are endeavoring to find a basis for the interchange of members, and are cultivating a sense of oneness in the native mind, preparatory to that actual union which they pray may come. The problems of baptism and the form of church government present the most formidable obstacles.

The most significant of all union movements, however, has been brought to successful conclusion in South India, the oldest of all mission fields, and the scene of the greatest missionary successes offered in lands where there is a native culture. It is the most significant because it is the first complete unification of different denominational bodies yet effected on a large scale, and because it gives promise of what other mission fields may do as they grow older and more mature in their native conceptions of Christianity.

Previous to 1907 the various Congregational bodies in South India united into one organic communion. In that year they invited the Presbyterian bodies to affiliate with them. The overture was accepted, and release was asked from the synod of the Presbyterian Church of India. This was granted, and a union church of 140,000 members was organized under the name of the South India United Church. Negotiations are now being carried on with the German Reformed and Lutheran bodies working in that section, and there are signs of promise that not only they, but, in course of time, all bodies of Christians in South India will come into the union, and there will be one simple Christian Church that will rank in members with many of the Christian communions at home.

The Edinburgh Commission on Co-operation and Union found many difficulties in the way of actual organic union, but declared that somewhere beneath them all must be found the deeper unities and the true spirit of Christ, in which alone we can answer his prayer for union.

4. THE DAY OF OPPORTUNITY.

That eminent missionary statesman, John R. Mott, in his recent book entitled, "The Decisive Hour of Christian Missions," says that in the face of the opportunities of to-day, overlapping, waste, and friction on the mission field are sinful. He contends that the question of union is not primarily doctrinal, but moral. God holds the church responsible for the conquest of the world, and if she allows the victory to wait and men to be lost while she bickers over traditions and opinions and politics, she is morally guilty of a recreancy to opportunity. Mr. Mott says, "The hope of real success in taking the gospel to all the non-Christian world in our day is in a campaign characterized by the spirit of unity." If the church were one, as the Master prayed, the world would soon be led to believe. Instead of millions wasted in duplicating plants for church work at home, it could be sent where the need was greatest. Villages with five churches could be well provided with edifices, be ministered unto by a much better type of preaching, pay more adequate salaries, and send as much as they keep for home work to the more needy tasks of the foreign field. Great city congregations that build magnificent edifices on opposite corners and spend tens of thousands on competing orators and choirs could make every slum and foreign quarter of the city a missionary parish, and then send tens of thouasnds to those who never heard the gospel they hold in common but follow in division. Money spent on denominational establishments for the sake of specific sectarian propaganda would reach a multitude with a healing hand where it opens wounds of discord in the body of Christ here at home. The missionary is less concerned about the things that divide. Christ is all in all to him because the need is so great and Christ alone is sufficient. Hudson Taylor said the China Inland Mission "regarded it of secondary importance by whom the sheaves were garnered." "Our divisions inflict serious wounds on the body of Christ," said a missionary at the Edinburgh Conference. But union will never come by conference or by platform; it will come by the overpowering force of a great objective. When the church sees the world as its Master saw it, they will unite for the specific purpose of saving it to his manner of life.

Opportunity calls for a conservation of forces. Never before were such openings offered. All the world is now practically explored, and with the opening of Tibet and Afghanistan the last of the closed lands are opened. There are regions in the Soudan where fanaticism would protest and doubtless make its martyrs, but that it can be entered is already proven. Vast areas of Central Asia are yet not pre-empted, but the work in Manchuria could be duplicated in many places there. The great Moslem world is yielding to a more tolerant attitude, and in Russia, Persia, and Turkey, Mohammedans are willing to listen to the Christian message. "Religion has been the cause of race hatreds and individual hatreds, but now we are learning that religion may be, and is the greatest band to bind us together into a great fellowship in the Fatherhood of a common God," said one of the leaders of New Turkey. Christianity should take the bond of unity to a man like that. Korea is reaping the greatest returns of any field open to-day, but there are millions not won in Korea, and nothing could so discourage the native church as a spirit of divisiveness or the competition of denominational enterprise for their fealty. Siam is as open as Korea, and Madagascar is again under the rule of a favorable governor. All Africa is ready for a Pentecost if only a generation of time be given and an army of efficient men and women be sent. China is so accessible that a prominent missionary there says no land is more open; it is certainly more tolerant and open to a free message to-day than Russia. Japan has passed through her era of reaction and opposition and is yielding as never before; the church made a gain of 70% there in the last decade. The ferment in India will issue in a new interest in the larger things of the world, and Christianity will reap a great harvest; already there is an unsurpassed opportunity to garner among the 50,000,000 low and out-castes and to compete with Islam for their fealty. Among the aboriginal tribes of West China there have been great ingatherings, but to introduce a divided church among them would be to hinder them and lose many. There is no way to answer this call of the cross adequately except by a united effort. John Mott believes that a union of forces to-day would double the effectiveness of the host upon the field; it would certainly more than double the power of the church at home to occupy the territory open.

The peoples of the earth are to-day awakened by the new internationalism. The victory of Japan over Russia, the peaceful revolution of China and Turkey, the vast spread of commerce, the awakening that the missionary has taken into every quarter of the globe, the quickened means of transportation, the railways into the heart of Africa and China and across Arabia, the recognition of the Orient in international conferences, the unrest of India, the opening of the great Soudan by England and France, the drawing of the nations together in The Hague Tribunal, the universal dissemination of cheap literature, the new peace and the promised prosperity of South America, and the universal progress of democracy in all the nations have opened the minds of men as they have never been opened before. Old prejudices and provincialism are on the wane and a larger view of the world is becoming universal. The spirit of national independence is growing among subject peoples, learning is becoming universalized, and science is spreading its evangelism of fact where superstition has reigned; all too often learning has taken with it a spurious and short-visioned skepticism, and commerce a materialism that will be difficult to uproot, once it is well attached to a people. Wars may arise in the friction that comes with a new found independence, racial hatreds will grow as subject races cultivate patriotism and a sense of independence, the customary haughtiness of a "superior" race will be resented by the rising of "inferior" peoples, and unless there is a gospel of peace to spread an effective evangel, trouble will be an inevitable accompaniment of the new age. If the nations and peoples are allowed to open minds to the larger world and to judge it by its past treatment of them, and by the spirit of the trader and politician alone, there can be only resentment in their hearts; but if there can be sown in their hearts the message of humanity, the truth of Christianity as distinct from the acts of so-called Christian men and nations, the confidence it gives every man in the better nature of himself and of his fellow-man, and the inspiring facts that history has to tell the unbiased mind of its contributions to the evolution of civilization, the new world that is to come may be born without the birthpangs of medievalism, and the evangel of

232

Faculty of Nankin University. This illustrates not only how different communions can co-operate in missionary work, but how different races labor side by side in it.

peace will become the harbinger of a true internationalism founded upon brotherly love.

The native church on the mission field desires
union. It will be a sad blow to its future effectiveness if we insist on drilling it in our traditions and set-
ting its plastic life firmly into our Western moulds.
Mr. Chang Ching-Yi, one of the leaders of the native
Chinese church, said at the Edinburgh Conference:
"Speaking plainly, we hope to see in the near future
a united Christian church without any denominational
distinctions. It is not your particular denomination
that you are working for, but for the establishment
of the Church of Christ in China." "I can conceive
of no figure of speech that will justify division of the
church," said J. Campbell Gibson, of China, one of the
greatest of living missionaries; "the church is the body
of Christ in Scriptural figure, and to divide it is to
rend it and to give it pain and to destroy its usefulness." The great tasks of evangelism and the planting
of both Christian character and Christian philanthropy in the mission field is to be largely the work
of the native church. What could be more disastrous
than to divide the forces and set them in competition;
what more wasteful than to leave them a spirit of con-
tention, and what less of the spirit of Christ than to
turn their minds against one another when millions
await their united efforts. The call of the time is
that the evangel shall be effective, that the day be
hastened, and that the native church be panoplied
with the instruments of a holy warfare, and not burdened down with the useless weapons of tradition,
Western opinion, or any sort of divisiveness.

If it was the desire of the Savior's heart that the nations should be at peace, we shall best lead them if we are united; if it was his desire that they should have his gospel and his prayer that his disciples be one that the world might believe, we shall best serve him by at least refraining from carrying our divisions to the mission field; if it be our own desire that the church be in that unity that will make it effective in the world and pleasing to its great head, we shall best realize our desire by enlisting the churches in the overwhelming task of bringing the world into his Kingdom. It will cost the sacrifice that every great quest costs, but no truth will be sacrificed, only our half-truths. It will be realized only as we forget self in the mighty crusade.

5. THE CALL OF THE CROSS.

What we call the Lord's Prayer was really the disciple's prayer. The real Lord's Prayer is that final petition which comes to us like a call from the cross. It was that we might all be one that the world might believe that he was sent. It was not a prayer for mere unity and co-operation. It was that we might be one, even as he and the Father were one. It was for a real and organic unity. It was that the union which characterized his disciples at that moment might always prevail. A divided church will never conquer a world. In the early days of the Reformation the leaders openly preached that missions were God's business, not ours. They were interested in speculative theologies, and thought more of correct definitions than of evangelizing a world. They thought the doctrine must be formulated properly or there could be no salvation. Luther denounced Zwingli in terms which burned with terror because the Swiss reformer differed from him in regard to the Lord's Supper. They had not learned with Christ that to do the will of God was the divine way of learning the true doctrine. Religion was more concerned with political affairs than with world-wide missions, and it was freely taught that the only missionary obligation was that resting upon governments in their colonial administrations. Good theologians frankly denounced the heathen as unworthy of salvation and called some who tried to take the gospel to them insane fanatics. As a result there was no missionary work of importance during the first two centuries after the beginning of the Reformation, but there were a number of divisions brought into the church, and the spirit that each sect maintained toward the other was anything but that of their divine Lord in his prayer for their union. That we are not yet purged of that ecclesiastical spirit all must acknowledge. We shall be under the incubus of it for some time no doubt, for there will be narrow-minded partisans, and even leaders who will be more devoted to their sect than to the Kingdom of God, until the spirit of fraternity so sweeps over the church that it carries them off their feet and hastens them along with a providential tide.

That day is fast approaching when the spirit of brotherhood will so seize upon the Church of Christ that there will be few apologists left for sectarianism and partisanship. The whole tide in the affairs of men is toward greater unity. Nations are merging from separated states into more closely annealed unities, as witness in our own country, Germany, China, India, Australia, and South Africa. The whole world is drawing together. The cable and telegraph, the swift locomotive and express steamship, wireless and the aeroplane, are abolishing distances and making all the world acquainted. Intelligence of one another brings understanding and abolishes prejudices. Trade and travel are welding us together with the metallic bonds of common interest. War was once pleaded for as a maker of trade and a creator of virile manhood. To-day commercial bodies are foremost in denouncing it as a destroyer of trade, and sociologists as the greatest devastator of the strength of nations. But a little while ago, as history records time, nations preyed upon one another, and all the world believed that to the strong belonged the battle. To-day no nation enters an imperialistic campaign without attempting to convince all the world that it is in the interests of the weaker peoples and for the good of the conquered. The interests of humanity are becoming one, and men are recognizing that co-operation between nations and peoples redound to mutual benefit, and that strife is both expensive and uncivilized.

What is happening between the nations is taking place within the nations. Co-operation is the watchword of both industry and commerce. Cut-throat competition is expensive and must die the death of all survivals of our barbaric life. Men have found that they can make more for themselves by agreeing together than by trying to get the advantage of one another. Labor is discovering that in unity lies its

236

only hope of a better wage and a higher standard of living. Co-operation is the watchword of the age, and it registers a new era in human progress.

This spirit of the age is nowhere more manifest than in the church. Every city has its evangelical alliance, or some organization that corresponds to it. Several States have church federations, and the Federal Council of Churches is equaled only by the English Free Church Council in the magnitude of its meaning as a unifier of Christian activities. There are few apologists for sectarianism left, and pulpits ring eloquently with union appeals in the name of the common faith we profess and the common task we have to do. In Canada, South Africa, and Australia genuine church union movements are in progress. In South Africa a temporary halt has been called, but in Canada the churches concerned are voting two to one for the merger, and the same majority obtains in Australia. In the United States the various Northern Baptist bodies are uniting, as are also the Presbyterians, and all denominations are conducting negotiations across the mythical Mason's and Dixon's line in an effort to overcome the unfortunate breaks brought on by the Civil War. The same process of first drawing together the denominational families into the larger denominational unity is operating at home as on the mission field. Where they lead we are sure to follow. We have the great incubus of tradition, lesser zeal, and the vested interests of denominational societies to deter us, but awakening missionary interest will imbue us with the same spirit that has been moving the real missionaries.

The most promising sign of the times, however, is the universal awakening of the church to its social duty. It has moved out of the down-town as the slum moved in, and the efforts of the social settlements to do what it would not undertake is rebuking it for social negligence. It has seen every form of social amelioration undertaken by organizations of Christians, organized under other names but seldom under her auspices, and she is asking why she has been unable to meet the need herself. The answer is her divisions. She has been taxed to support duplicating church organizations and had nothing left, either of money or men, to devote to the greater task of social effort. She has unsparingly denounced Roman Catholic ecclesiastical and doctrinal errors, but been compelled to see a united Catholic church rebuke her with a charity that is unexampled, and she realizes that it is not Catholic doctrine but Catholic unity that has made it possible, while it is not Protestant doctrine but Protestant divisiveness that has prevented her from doing it. The late Amory Bradford said that he found in one town in Japan four little Methodist missions, each of which had to be visited by a different bishop from home, representing the sub-denominational divisions we maintained, and the expense was paid by contributions taken in pleas for the heathen. The mission churches saw the irony of such a condition, and those four missions are to-day one, with their own native bishop to superintend their work. When the churches at home awaken to an economic sense of the waste involved in denominational duplication, they will stop it on the home mission field as they are already stopping it on the foreign field. "Denominationalism, as a principle, is doomed to death," says Canon Hensley Henson, a noted Anglican clergyman. It will not be undone in a day, for as Robert Speer says, "From the beginning the greatest evils have succeeded in rooting themselves in the consciences of men," nor will it be done by ecclesiastical procedure, but by the overwhelming power of a great objective, such as the conversion of the world and the bringing in of the Kingdom of God.

Missionaries are tremendously impressed with the social needs of the world. They make their homes social settlements, and adopt institutional methods in their churches. They wrestle with the larger social problems in their active ministries and grapple with the social evils of heathenism with firm and steady hands. "The message for China," says Frank Garrett, of Nanking, Secretary of the Evangelistic Council for China, "is the message of the prophets, justice and righteousness and God's protecting care. The message of Amos rings out as though it were written for China to-day. What China needs to-day is men of the type of the old prophets of Israel. The leading men in the Chinese ministry to-day preach a social and national message." Just because this larger conception of the work of the Kingdom of God has seized hold upon them, they have less interest in perpetuating divisions. Fraternity is the great social message that Christians must bear to the mission fields, and they can not do it well with a divided church. They can not preach the full gospel while their hearers are asking why they are divided, if there is but one Christ and one way of salvation. So the missionaries in Japan have declared that "all who are one in Christ by faith are one body," and those in China have united in the declaration that "in planting the Church of Christ on Chinese soil, we desire only to plant one church under the sole control of the Lord Jesus Christ." In Korea and the Philippines the missions, with one exception, all wear one name and banish the denominational title to a parenthesis that can be easily erased.

The call of the Cross is a call to united service in the interests of all humanity and of all that benefits humanity. Christ said more about this world than any other founder of a great religion. He did not neglect the other, nor can we long keep a message for this present age if we have not one for the future, but his emphasis was upon the need of righteousness. Men were to believe unto righteousness; they were to seek God and his righteousness; his Kingdom was one of righteousness, and he died that men might become righteous. To do justly, love mercy, and walk humbly with God is the world's great social need. Religion only can constrain it to such ends, and Christianity offers the divine prescription through its Lord. When the Christian world is more concerned about living Christ than it is about defining him, it will come to understand him, but never until then. The missionary faces the mighty forces of heathenism and is enlisted in service against them. He sees the need of a solid front and is leading Christendom into that union, both with its Lord and with one another, for which

he prayed as he went to the cross to lay down his life
for the world.

> And what dost thou answer Him, O my soul?
> Is it nothing to thee as the ages roll,
> That the Lord of Life should suffer in vain,
> That He who was Prince in the Realm of Pain,
> Should seek for the sin-stricken children of men,
> That by way of the cross He might bring them again
> To the fold of His care—His infinite care,
> That thou shouldst turn from this, His prayer,
> And deaden thine ear to His wondrous plea,
>   The call of the Christ to me?
>   —*By Claude Kelly, in Missions.*

APPENDIX

BIBLIOGRAPHY

The following list of books is selected from among those consulted in the preparation of this volume:

Dennis. (Jas. S.) Christian Missions and Social Progress. Three Vols. Revell.

Mackenzie. (W. D.) Christianity and the Progress of Man. Revell.

Keen. (W. R.) The Service of Missions to Science and Philanthropy. Baptist Missionary Union.

Grant. (W. H.) Philanthropy in Missions. Foreign Missions Library, New York.

Tenny. (E. P.) Contrasts in Social Progress. Longmans.

Stevenson. (R. T.) The Missionary Interpretation of History. Jennings & Graham.

Mott. (J. R.) The Decisive Hour of Christian Missions. Student Volunteer Movement.

Lindsay. (A. R. B.) Gloria Christi. Macmillans.

Montgomery. (H. B.) Western Women in Eastern Lands. Macmillans.

Slater. (T. E.) Missions and Sociology. Elliot Stock. London.

Bryan. (W. J.) Letters to a Chinese Official. McClure & Phillips.

Speer. (R. E.) Christianity and the Nations. Revell.

Speer. (R. E.) Missions and Modern History. Revell.

APPENDIX

Osgood. (Dr. E. I.) Breaking Down Chinese Walls. Revell.

Hunt. (W. R.) Heathenism Under the Searchlight. Morgan & Scott. London.

Faust. (A. K.) Christianity as a Social Factor in Japan. University of Pennsylvania.

Allan. (G. A.) Civilization and Foreign Missions. Elliot Stock. London.

Fowler. (C. H.) Missions and World Movements. Jennings & Graham.

Williamson. (J. R.) The Healing of the Nations. Student Volunteer Movement.

Edwards. (M. R.) The Work of the Medical Missionary. Student Volunteer Movement.

Russel. (Norman.) Village Work in India. Revell.

Lewis. (R. E.) The Educational Conquest of the Far East. Revell.

Brown. (A. J.) New Forces in Old China. Revell.

Crafts. (W. E.) Temperance Argument on a Missionary Background. The Reform Bureau.

Griffis. (W. E.) Verbeck of Japan. Revell.

Report of the Edinburgh Missionary Conference. Vols. II, III, VIII.

Chang Chi Tung. China's Only Hope. Revell.

Stewart. (J. R.) Dawn in the Dark Continent. Revell.

Hepburn. (J. D.) Twenty Years in Khama's Country. Hodder & Stoughton.

Chalmers. (Jas.) Pioneer Life and Work in New Guinea. Revell.

Griffis. (W. E.) A Maker of the New Orient. Revell.

APPENDIX

Dye. (Eva N.) Bolenge. Foreign Christian Missionary Society.

Clark. (W. N.) A Study of Christian Missions. Scribners.

Clark. (J. B.) Leavening the Nation. Baker & Taylor.

Weir. (Samuel.) Christianity and Civilization. Eaton & Mains.

Brace. (Loring.) Gesta Christa. A. & C. Armstrong.

Scmidt. (C.) The Social Results of Early Christianity. Isbester. London.

Uhlhorn. (Gerhardt.) Christian Charity in the Early Church. Scribners.

Nash. (H. S.) The Genesis of the Social Conscience. Macmillan.

Kidd. (Benj.) Social Evolution. Macmillan.

Patten. (S. N.) The Social Basis of Religion. Macmillan.

Freemantle. (W. H.) The World as the Subject of Redemption. Longmans.

CLASS QUESTIONS.

INTRODUCTION.

SECTION 1.

By what means would Jesus save the world?

In what does personality consist? What relation does it bear to the work of missions?

What is the Kingdom of God? What do we mean by "saving the world?"

Discriminate between a theological and sociological Christianity.

In what way does the work of missions influence the social life of a people?

Discuss missions as a factor in creating a civilization.

SECTION 2.

How does the missionary overthrow false and cruel custom?

Contrast the average of social life in paganism and Christianity.

Must a people adopt western customs to become Christians?

Can a people be transformed and made independent by the external gifts of civilization alone? Why is the "creation of new desires" fundamental?

Contrast a heathen with a Christian village.

Enumerate some of the social tasks of missions.

Discuss the relation of missionary work to social progress.

SECTION 3.

Which religions have been missionary and which not?

Wherein do Confucianism and Buddhism lack social force? What in Mohammedanism makes it anti-social?

Compare the missionary motive and success of Christianity to those of other great religions.

What has been the secret of Christianity's success as a missionary religion?

What is the effect of missionary work on the moral standards of (1) individuals? (2) society?

Discuss Christianity in comparison with other religions as a universal faith.

248

APPENDIX

CHAPTER I.

SECTION 1.

What is the final test of a culture or a religion?

Which religion has done most to forward progress? Name some of the fundamentals it contributes to social progress.

Why is paganism pessimistic and Christianity optimistic?

Relate wherein each of the great non-Christian religions have fallen short as forces for social progress.

How do pre-Christian civilizations compare to Christian civilizations?

How account for the difference?

Discuss the secret of social progress in Christian civilizations.

SECTION 2.

Why should missionary statistics be interesting?

Is Christianity the original faith of any people? What in its history justifies the belief that it will become the religion of all peoples?

Relate the progress of missionary work in each of the great missionary fields. Give the figures that show the total progress of the missionary conquest.

Enumerate some of the accomplishments of missions that figures can not tell.

How does the generosity of mission churches compare with that of the churches at home? What progress is missionary interest making at home?

Discuss the interest of the church in its world-wide task.

SECTION 3.

What makes Christianity the most virile factor in social progress?

What is the difference between a negative and a positive statement of the Golden Rule?

Wherein do the great non-Christian religions fail as leavens for social progress?

How does the personality of Christ contribute to the social power of Christianity?

What is meant by "the sacrifice of service?" How does the missionary illustrate it?

Discuss the nature of Christianity as a social leaven.

SECTION 4.

What was the social status of our Teutonic ancestors before the missionary went to them?

APPENDIX

What can you say of democracy in Greece? Of the status
of woman? Of children? Of slaves in Rome?

What fundamental power in Christianity has always preserved it?

In what social state did the missionary find the various
peoples of Europe? How long did it take to transform
them? How does the progress of missionary work in
China and Japan compare to that made in Britain,
Germany, and other historical lands?

Discuss the comparative progress of modern missions.

SECTION 5.

What evangelistic power is found in ideas?

What idea is incarnate in the missionary?

What particular phase of missionary work is winning the
approval of publicists and statesmen? Why?

In what does the missionary found progress? What relation does spiritual transformation bear to material
progress in his work?

How does the conversion of individuals to Christianity
react upon society?

Discuss the force of ideas as compared with the force of arms as
a factor in the civilizing process.

CHAPTER II.

SECTION 1.

What relation must exist between husband and wife to make
a true home?

What place does the Koran give woman?

What part does the family meal play in a Christian and in
a pagan home?

How does the position of woman in heathenism compare to
that given her in Christian lands?

What mars the patriarchial household as a home?

What can you say of divorce in non-Christian lands?

What emphasis does the missionary put upon the home?

Discuss the Christian home in comparison with the heathen.

SECTION 2.

What position was accorded woman in Greece and Rome?
Among the Teutons?

What place did early Christianity give her? Under what
emperors was she first given greater legal rights?

Enumerate the gifts of Christianity to her.

Discuss the relation of "woman's rights" to progress in history.

APPENDIX

State the position of woman in non-Christian lands to-day as compared with her position in pre-Christian Europe.

Describe the lot of Hindu widows. What position do the Chinese give woman? The Moslems? What is her status in savage society? To what extent is education given girls in pagan lands to-day?

Why are women slowest to accept Christianity?

Why have the Parsis failed to give India their ideals for women?

Discuss the comparative status of womankind in Christian and non-Christian lands to-day.

SECTION 4.

How does the pagan and Christian ideal for child life compare?

What was "exposure" of children in Rome?

What legal rights do non-Christian governments usually accord children?

How widespread was the pagan practice of infanticide?

What guarantee of right does Christianity alone accord children?

Discuss the influence of the missionary upon child life.

SECTION 5.

What is the social settlement idea?

How does the missionary home become a settlement? How many missionary homes are there? Tell some of the concrete ways in which the missionary home conveys Christianity to its neighbors.

Describe some examples of heathen homes and villages. Contrast with them those of native Christians.

What are the main influences of the missionary home?

Discuss the missionary home as a social settlement.

CHAPTER III.

SECTION 1.

What part does benevolence play in social progress?

What can you say for the benevolences of paganism?

What is the average economic condition in non-Christian lands? What result does drouth or flood bring?

Enumerate some of the inhuman practices of heathenism. What change does the missionary bring?

Discuss "the struggle for others" as a factor in human progress.

251

APPENDIX

SECTION 2.

What relation does healing hold to missionary work? What use did Jesus make of it?

What effect does physical depression have on moral life?

Why does the medical missionary so easily get a hearing?

Why did Buddhism lose its primitive charity?

Enumerate the larger influences of the medical missionary.

Discuss the value of medical missions to missionary work.

SECTION 3.

What is the state of scientific knowledge in China? India? Japan? Africa?

Enumerate some of the medical practices of non-scientific lands.

How does the death rates compare in Christian and non-Christian lands?

What is the fruitful source of disease in non-Christian lands?

What treatment is accorded the insane and lepers in non-Christian lands?

Discuss the value of scientific knowledge to missionary work.

SECTION 4.

How adequately are the medical needs of missionary lands met?

Describe the extent of medical practice under missionary auspices.

What use does the medical missionary make of preventive measures? Give instances of phenomenal clinics.

What does he do in the way of founding a native medical profession? Enumerate instances. When will his work be done?

Discuss the influence of the medical missionary upon social progress.

SECTION 5.

Relate instances where medical missions have opened doors. Why is the physician more able to do this than others?

Tell how he enlists native benevolence. Give instances.

Describe the pervasiveness of medical work; the way in which it cultivates native sympathy.

What peculiar work can the woman physician do?

Give ex-Secretary Foster's estimate of the value of medical missions.

Discuss the evangelistic value of missionary benevolence.

252

APPENDIX

CHAPTER IV.

SECTION 1.

What use does the missionary make of education? Give statistics of missionary schools.

Enumerate some missionary contributions to the literature of non-Christian lands.

How extensively does he supply schools? What does he teach in them? Why should he give a general education?

What is the educational status in non-Christian lands?

Relate the progress of education in Japan and China.

What is the fundamental thing in education? How does the mission school supply it in comparison with the governmental school of a non-Christian land? What is the difference between a governmental school in a non-Christian land and a public school in a Christian land in the teaching of morals?

Discuss the place of Christian education in civilization.

SECTION 2.

What dangers do mere material gifts take to inferior civilizations?

How does Christian education supply the fundamental elements in a civilizing process?

Cite instances of missionary education furnishing native leadership.

What is the extent of the influence of educated Christian men in Japan? in China? What handicap are they under in China? Why?

What influence does Christianity have on the making of a democracy?

What was Gladstone's test of a religion's efficiency?

Discuss the place of native leadership in the progress of a people.

SECTION 3.

Is the primitive mind practical? What of its scientific habits? Why does the Malaysian refuse to earn wages?

What fundamental does industrial training supply the primitive mind in the creation of social progress?

What is the ideal of industrial training in mission schools?

Relate instances where industrial training has created industrial communities.

What fundamental economic factor does civilization supply? How does industrial training make it effective?

How does industrial education react upon the direct purpose of the missionary in his evangelistic work?

Discuss the place of industrial habits in social progress.

APPENDIX

Describe the state of female education in China, Japan, India, Africa.

Contrast Christian and pagan ideals of education.

What is the fundamental necessity for educating womankind?

What is the practical necessity of all missionary education? How applied to the education of girls?

How does an educated womanhood affect pagan social customs?

Discuss the value of educated mothers to the race.

SECTION 5.

Relate instances where missionary schools have been effective evangelizing agencies.

What effect does missionary education have upon the Moslem mind? Can it be called an evangelistic agency among them?

What is an "evangelism of preparation?"

How does the school appeal to the educated caste of a pagan land?

What educational necessity rests upon missions in making an effective native church?

Discuss the reaction of environment upon the evangelistic work of missions.

CHAPTER V.

SECTION 1.

Contrast the motives and benefits brought to a pagan society by the trader, soldier, missionary.

What is the community influence of the missionary and how does he exercise it?

Contrast the results of paternalism and those of a training in the arts of democracy.

Does white contact necessarily result in the decimation of native races? What kind of contact decimates? What kind elevates?

By what means does missionary influence affect the larger political, social, and commercial life of a people?

Discuss the civilizing power of the missionary in contrast to those of trade, war, and politics.

SECTION 2.

Are there any democracies among non-Christian governments? What type of rule prevails among them? How is justice administered?

APPENDIX

Quote various authorities on missionary influence in political progress.

Give instances of direct missionary work and influence in transforming the political life of a people.

What indirect influence does missionary work have on the political life of a people?

Discuss the influence of the missionary in the evolution of modern government in mission lands.

SECTION 3.

What is meant by "making two blades of grass grow where one grew before?"

What is the difference between "planting" and "rescuing" as a missionary program?

What part does the creation of new wants play in social progress? Relate how missionary work stimulates them and give instances of how the missionary has supplied them.

Narrate instances where he has become a "captain of industry."

What fundamental moral sense does he inject into trade and industry?

Discuss the relation of missionary work to material progress.

SECTION 4.

Enumerate ways in which the missionary becomes the pioneer of civilization. How does his work contribute to trade and commerce?

In what is the work of the trader inimical to missionary work? Give instances of conflict between them.

How does the missionary prepare a people for the innovations of civilization?

Enumerate examples of missionary trading companies. What financial relation does the missionary hold to them? What special work do they do?

What special missionary enterprise is advocated by Dr. Josiah Strong? Would it be effective as a social influence?

Discuss the value of increased earning power to the higher arts of civilization.

SECTION 5.

Enumerate instances of international agreements, conferences, and federations.

Name some of the things that make against warfare in our time.

APPENDIX

Narrate how the nations are "preparing for war in times of peace." Who pays the bills finally?

What two things have been the chief causes of modern war? Have missionaries ever directly brought on a war? What of the Boxer rebellion?

Enumerate instances where the missionary has brought about peace.

What faith does the missioner have in the potentiality of the least of men? What attitude of mind does he cultivate that makes for peace?

Discuss the missionary as a factor in the uniting of the nations in bonds of comity and peace.

CHAPTER VI.

SECTION 1.

Give the number of unevangelized. What of the task among Moslems? In India? China? Japan? Africa? The unoccupied lands?

What particular promise does each of these missionary territories hold out?

What supreme call comes to the churches in face of the task?

Discuss the advantage of union among the churches for the sake of evangelizing the world.

SECTION 2.

What are the forces that make for Christian union?

What gave rise to the various denominations? Do the original causes still obtain?

Is there an advantage or disadvantage in divisions on the mission field? What advantage in union? How do our home divisions hinder unity on the mission field?

Enumerate spheres of work in which co-operation is found easy.

Give the great fundamentals on which all churches agree.

Discuss the practicability of a union of churches on the mission field.

SECTION 3.

What force will bring union? What is meant by an "overpowering common objective?" What are the first steps to union?

Enumerate the great standing conferences of missionaries: The permanent Boards of Arbitration.

Tell of the Methodist and Presbyterian division of the field in Korea. What approach to union is found in West China? In India?

APPENDIX

Enumerate instances of a union support of schools; of union within great denominational families.

What specific efforts are being made for "geographical union?" Tell of the South India United Church.

Discuss the "overpowering common objective" as a means to Christian union.

SECTION 4.

What is John R. Mott's judgment on the question of unity?

What economic gain would come to missionary work through union?

Enumerate specific opportunities that call for a conservation of forces. What notable modern movements are opening work and preparing the way? What great need of a gospel of peace?

Why should the native church be a united church? What sacrifice will it cost the church at home?

Discuss the value of a united versus a divided native church.

SECTION 5.

Is the intent of the Savior's prayer for unity or for actual union?

What was the attitude of the early leaders in the Reformation toward missions?

Enumerate ways in which the world-wide spirit of unity is manifesting itself. How is it manifesting itself in the churches at home? What are the chief deterrents?

How have divisions hindered the church in doing social work? How would union help? Contrast Catholicism and Protestantism in the direct work of financing philanthropic enterprises. Why is the former strongest in it?

What demand does social progress upon the mission field make upon the church? Is the church awakening to its social duty? What effect will it have upon Christian union?

Discuss the social work of Christianity as a force making for Christian union.

INDEX

AND

CROSS REFERENCE INDEX.

(The italicized words constitute a cross reference index.)

INDEX

INDEX

INDEX

INDEX

INDEX

INDEX

264

INDEX

DATE DUE

NOV 2 4 2010	

DEMCO, INC. 38-2931